WHO OWNS THE CORPORATION?
MANAGEMENT VS. SHAREHOLDERS

A Twentieth Century Fund Paper

WHO OWNS THE CORPORATION?

Management vs. Shareholders

BY EDWARD JAY EPSTEIN

 Priority Press Publications/New York/1986

The Twentieth Century Fund is a research foundation undertaking timely analyses of economic, political, and social issues. Not-for-profit and nonpartisan, the Fund was founded in 1919 and endowed by Edward A. Filene.

BOARD OF TRUSTEES OF THE TWENTIETH CENTURY FUND

Morris B. Abram
H. Brandt Ayers
Peter A. A. Berle, *Chairman*
José A. Cabranes
Joseph A. Califano, Jr.
Alexander Morgan Capron
Edward E. David, Jr.
Brewster C. Denny
Charles V. Hamilton
August Heckscher, Emeritus
Matina S. Horner
James A. Leach

Georges-Henri Martin
Lawrence K. Miller, Emeritus
P. Michael Pitfield
Don K. Price, Emeritus
Richard Ravitch
Arthur M. Schlesinger, Jr.
Albert Shanker
Harvey I. Sloane, M.D.
Theodore C. Sorensen
James Tobin
David B. Truman, Emeritus
Shirley Williams

M. J. Rossant, *Director*

Copyright © 1986 by the Twentieth Century Fund, Inc.
Manufactured in the United States of America.
ISBN: 0-87078-208-8

Foreword

The big corporation is a subject of continuing fascination. It was more than fifty years ago that Berle and Means, in their classic study *The Modern Corporation and Private Property*, demonstrated that managers in their executive suites, rather than shareholders, control the levers of corporate power. Since that time, corporations have enjoyed enormous growth, abroad as well as domestically, despite the efforts of government to exercise some restraint on their operations. But if corporations cannot be controlled by shareholders or restrained by government, they have become increasingly vulnerable to hostile takeover attempts by a relatively small group of rapacious raiders who, with the benefit of financial leverage, have managed to create something close to panic in the executive suites of the corporations that they have targeted for attack.

Not that corporate executives lack defenses. In the past few years, the public, including the share-owning public, has been witness to the unseemly spectacle of raiders making bids for corporations and corporate managers engrossed in carrying out preventive tactics—ranging from golden parachutes that cushion their exits in the event of defeat to green mail and poison pills and all the other euphemisms for strategies that pillage the resources of the corporation—in order to maintain their positions. No consideration is given on either side to corporate employees. Nor is any heed given to the shareholders who are the presumed owners of the corporation. Instead, both the raiders and the defenders, with their phalanxes of investment bankers, lawyers, and accountants, concentrate all their attention on trying to best each other, making sure that they come out ahead.

Edward Jay Epstein has examined the current wave of takeovers in this paper for the Fund. An analytical writer, the author of *Inquest*, the classic study of the Warren Commission's report on the assassination of John F. Kennedy, as well as articles and books on intelligence operations and the workings of the media, he makes plain his view that shareholders, especially the individual investor, are almost always the losers in these battles for control. They have been effectively disenfranchised, reduced to mere onlookers in corporate struggles, helpless to protect themselves against entrenched management or the calculating raider, both of whom are intent on the cavalier use of shareholder assets to finance their careers. The individual shareholder rarely gets the premium that raiders are prepared to pay for control. And they are not the recipients of the green mail that managements are prepared to pay, with corporate funds, to fend off raiders.

Such antics are not making corporations more competitive or more profitable. Instead, they are an irresponsible though immensely rewarding exercise, diverting both funds and intellectual energy from basic corporate purposes. They may enrich a comparative few but at what expense to the many and to the nation? Whether or not the specific reforms that Epstein proposes will curb what has become an embarrassing excess of contemporary capitalism, his focus on the takeover mania should stimulate debate and, I hope, corrective action.

M. J. Rossant, DIRECTOR
The Twentieth Century Fund
October 1986

Contents

Foreword by M. J. Rossant — v

1 / The Myth of Corporate Democracy	1
2 / The Political Metaphor	7
3 / The Truth About Corporate Democracy: The Fallacy of Electoral Democracy	13
4 / The Poison Pill	31
5 / The Future of Ownerless Capitalism: A Worst-Case Scenario	41
6 / Redressing the Balance	43
Notes	47
Appendix A. Proxy Contests for 1984	51
Appendix B. Selected Green Mail Payments, 1979-1985	55
Appendix C. Selected Golden Parachute Payments, 1981-1985	61
Appendix D. Companies Adopting Poison Pills (8/7/86)	63

Acknowledgments

I gratefully acknowledge support for this paper from the Twentieth Century Fund. It benefited enormously from the research and analyses done by Edmund Levin. I would also like to thank Carey Hirtz and Eve Spencer of the Skadden Arps, Slate, Meagher and Flom Law Library, Deborah Gardner and Peter Eisenstadt of the New York Stock Exchange Archives, James E. Heard of the Investor Responsibility Research Center, and Marlene McHugh of the Fund staff for their generous assistance.

Finally, I want to thank Beverly Goldberg and M. J. Rossant of the Fund for the perceptive editing of the manuscript.

1 / The Myth of Corporate Democracy

The issue of who controls corporate America has been brought into focus recently by a series of extraordinary attempts to take over multibillion dollar companies. Mergers and acquisitions are, of course, hardly a new form of corporate activity. American corporations for at least the last thirty years have used them to increase their market share, diversify their risks, improve their balance sheets, or, not uncommonly, obtain a tax benefit. Until the 1980s, the vast preponderance of these mergers and acquisitions have been "friendly," or at least approved by the boards of directors of both parties, since state laws made unfriendly takeovers extremely difficult and potentially dangerous undertakings for corporations. The Illinois Business Take Over Act, for example, allowed state officials to intervene if 10 percent of the shareholders in a targeted company were residents of that state. When the Supreme Court struck down this statute in June 1982, it invalidated other similar state laws, radically changing the situation. By doing so, the Court made carrying out hostile raids much more feasible.[1]

Whereas conventional mergers and acquisitions, especially those undertaken by conglomerates, had the aim of increasing the size of the entity, even if they temporarily depressed the price of the shares, the new takeovers had the objective of shrinking the acquired company, by selling off its divisions, to enhance the price of its shares. In the former, the management of the acquired companies was usually incorporated into the conglomerate; in the latter, the management was replaced. In this sense, the new-style takeovers were hostile toward the management of the targeted companies—though not necessarily their share owners. The challenges tended to create a direct conflict of interest between management, which wanted to maintain, if not expand, its domain, and share owners, who wanted to increase the stock market value of their investments.

The ability of outside raiders to take over some of the largest and most established corporations in America—a possibility that was all but unthinkable before the 1980s—was greatly enhanced by two changes in government regulatory policy. First, antitrust law, which had served as a barrier to one corporation swallowing up another, was relaxed when applied to situations where competition was demonstrably diminished. Second, banking regulations, especially those governing banks and savings and loan associations, were revamped to allow these institutions more freedom in investing the savings entrusted to them. This second deregulation made huge pools of credit available for financing stock purchases. All that remained was for resourceful investment bankers, such as Drexel Burnham Lambert, to craft debt instruments to channel these funds to clients who would use them to make tender offers for controlling blocks of shares in established companies.

To complete the circle, this financing, usually in the form of newly created unrated debentures, dubbed "junk bonds," was backed by the very assets of the company that was the target of the raid. Through this financial alchemy, it became possible for individual investors, with comparatively little capital of their own, to use the funds from deregulated banks to bid for corporations with billions of dollars in assets. All that was necessary was for takeover entrepreneurs—or their investment bankers—to find companies whose shares were selling at substantially less than their asset value.

Since raiders almost always directed their tender offers to the share owners, and commonly conditioned them on their ability to wrest control from the existing managements, they threatened the careers and prestige of corporate officers. For the most part, these executives were not willing to cede their claims to corporate control and abandon their positions, with all of their perks, on the basis of what their nominal owners might decide to do with their shares. They thus attempted to prevent such offers, which they also may have doubted were in the best interest of the shareholder, by denying the shareholder the opportunity to sell his shares.

To this end, with the assistance of law firms that specialize in corporate defense, they adopted strategies with intriguing names that were designed to bribe or cajole the raider into abandoning his bid, such as "green mail" and "lollipops"; or that attempted to make the company less attractive, such as "scorched earth" and "crown jewel lockups," which involved selling off or optioning key assets; or that made it infeasible to merge with the company, such as "poison pills." If all else failed, they could attempt a friendly merger with a "white knight," or even buy the company themselves through a leveraged buy out. Law firms retained by the raiders spared no expense in fiercely challenging in court every defensive tactic employed by the besieged managements. The result of these pitched battles, in what Steve Brill of the *American Lawyer* described as the "roaring 1980s," was a thorough, if unintended, reexamination of the ways and means by which corporations are actually governed.

Whatever else these no-holds-barred contests accomplished, they stripped away much of the rhetorical tangle surrounding the participation of share owners in corporate affairs. The heat of these battles, involving legal bills in some cases of $50 million, often paid for by shareholders, generated sufficient light to expose large new gaps between the ownership and management of public corporations. The critical presumption made by the courts, Congress, and government agencies, as well as by investors and economists—that there were mechanisms that somehow ultimately made those who managed corporate wealth responsible to those who owned it—was called into question.

Out of this bitter debate emerged a sharp divergence of views on the purpose of the corporation in the American system of capitalism. Whereas many shareholders thought of it in terms of its profitability, corporate management tended to define it in terms of service to the community, suggesting that their corporations were "institutions," much like museums or hospitals, that served a public interest as well as the private interest of shareholders. While the purpose of these fights was to grasp, or keep, control over valuable assets, the effect, although an unintended effect, was to lift a huge rock that had obscured the way corporate governance really worked.

The issue at stake here transcends that of the legal rights of individual share owners. It concerns the way in which most of America's resources and industry are controlled. At the heart of the free enterprise system is the assumption that private owners of capital, guided only by the "invisible hand" of the marketplace, will invest the productive wealth of society more efficiently than governments or bureaucracies that do not act on the profit motive. The idea is that competition for the highest return on capital will force those who cannot use their capital efficiently—or imaginatively—to sell or rent it to others who can. Each small capitalist, motivated by nothing more than greed, thus will, without a grand design, help society use its total wealth in the best possible way. This economic vision, refined from the pin factory Adam Smith described in *The Wealth of Nations,* justifies the preference for a free market economy over a socialist system—or, in the nomenclature of the United Nations, a "centrally planned economy."

Whether or not these laissez-faire assumptions can be empirically proven, they have provided the rationale for much of public policy toward the economy. They have not only justified a hands-off policy toward business by the government and the courts, but also provided a basis for all the special tax incentives, employee stock-ownership plans, subsidies, and other dispensations meant to encourage widespread ownership of corporations.

These vital assumptions would be invalid if the corporations in which most of the nation's capital was vested were controlled not by their owners, intent on maximizing their profit, but by managerial bureaucracies perpetuating their own tenure in office. Given these circumstances, corporate executives, who could not be ousted by the owners, could not be presumed to have the same incentives as ones who could. Executives with such life tenure would have every reason to spend corporate revenues to enhance their own salaries, comfort, and standings in the community, and to continue unprofitable lines on which their friends and allies depended for their income or prestige, even though such expenditures reduced the return on capital. They would not be compelled by any sort of "invisible hand" to maximize the return on the capital entrusted to them. In purely economic terms, they would not have any more motivation to run their enterprise with maximum efficiency than would managers of quasi-public bureaucracies.

This was not a problem that Adam Smith or other laissez-faire economists had to reckon with, because in their time there was no meaningful distinction between the motives of owners and managers of capital. Those who owned a corporation could fire a manager who did not maximize the value of their property. In the United States, as late as 1890, there were fewer than seventy-five corporations in which the controlling blocks of shares were held either by a single entrepreneur, such as John D. Rockefeller, Andrew Mellon, or Andrew Carnegie; by a family trust, such as the DuPonts; or by a private bank, such as the House of Morgan. The so-called publicly owned corporation, in which management is separated from ownership and ownership is fragmented among many share owners, is really a phenomenon of the twentieth century that began during the stock boom of the 1920s.

The subsequent crash dispersed many large family-owned blocks, and, as the depression set in, more and more corporations were left without any dominant owner. In theory, shareholders appointed the boards of directors, which then hired the executives who ran these corporations.

In practice, however, the reverse took place: The executives managing the companies nominated themselves, or their supporters, to the board of directors, and then gave the shareholders no choice but to ratify their selections.

The growing tendency of management to seize and maintain control of American corporations was first demonstrated in 1932 by Adolph A. Berle, then a legal scholar at Columbia University. Based on the statistical analyses done by his colleague Gardiner C. Means, Berle showed in his classic study of the modern corporation that because of the overwhelming mass of complex information involved in the corporate form, management made all real decisions, including how the corporation was governed.

This managerial revolution had left the nonemployed owner little more than the role of passive shareholder.[2] As shareholders became increasingly more dispersed, with owners typically having only a minute fraction of the company, the status of shareholders was reduced to that of "absentee landlords."[3] Managers, moreover, could not be presumed to be motivated by the same economic logic as owners. Managers, for example, have a powerful pull to expand the company into other businesses to enhance their own power, prestige, or tenure—even though it diminishes the market value of the total investment. Owners, on the other hand, have an incentive to reduce the size of the company by selling assets that increase the value of their investment. After Berle, the issue was no longer who runs the modern corporation. It could be empirically shown that management does, without the participation of shareholders. The real issue was to whom, if anyone, is management ultimately accountable. Even absentee landlords can fire their managers.

While share owners grew progressively more demoralized by depressed stock prices in the 1930s, the New Deal administration became increasingly disposed to intervene in the economy by establishing government-run enterprises, such as the Tennessee Valley Authority, and by regulating the operations of banks and financial institutions. In this atmosphere, the separation between management and ownership, and the question of to whom it was accountable, had political as well as academic implications.

The response to this vexing problem, and the implicit threat of government intervention, was an attempt to apply the political model of representative government to corporate America. Managers would be made responsible to share owners through a democratic process of voting, just as representatives are responsible to citizens. To make this linkage more credible, the Securities and Exchange Commission (SEC), which had been created in 1934 to regulate stock transactions, imposed administrative rules on corporations that were designed to assure fair and timely elections for directors, as well as to make sure that the corporations disclosed all pertinent information to dissident shareholders. The rationale, which was based on the idea of corporate democracy, was that doing so would make publicly owned corporations answerable to the majority will of their electorates.

2 / The Political Metaphor

In short order, the political metaphor of corporate democracy became a vital part of the mythology of American capitalism. Shareholders were equated with voters; boards of directors with elected representatives; the principle of "one share, one vote" with universal suffrage; proxy solicitations with election campaigns; corporate charters and bylaws with constitutions and amendments; shareholder meetings with town meetings; the right of class action lawsuits with judicial review; and disclosure of corporate developments with a free press.

The form of corporate governance suggested by this metaphor is not, of course, tantamount to direct participation. Just as elected representatives of government do not necessarily poll their constituencies on each of their political decisions, corporate managers do not have to consult their shareholders on day-to-day business decisions. They merely have to run the enterprise in a way that satisfies their constituents. The underlying premise is that shareholders, like voters in a democracy, have the power to fire, or at least not reelect, managers who do not act in their interest.

Nor are the managers supposed to be motivated by altruism. As in the Burkean model of government, where representatives, good or bad by inclination, are forced to act in the interest of the electorate to keep their seats, corporate managers must act in the interest of the shareholders because their jobs depend on it. If managers do not perform satisfactorily, the shareholders will end their tenure in office, either by directly voting them out of office or by selling their shares to others who will then take over the corporation and replace the managers. In this theory, by forcing management to face shareholders in regular elections, the narrow self-interest of management in keeping the perks and prestige of its office is brought closer to the more general interest of shareholders—maximizing the value of their investment.

The myth of corporate democracy was further popularized by the New York Stock Exchange (NYSE) for self-serving reasons: to reassure the public and to thereby encourage the purchase of common stocks. As John J. Phelan, Jr., its chairman, testified in 1985, "The exchange's leadership in developing high standards of corporate democracy has played a major role in expanding public ownership in this country."[1] Although he traced the exchange's "pioneering effort"—which included requiring companies that were listed on the exchange to hold regular meetings, issue annual reports, and allow shareholders to vote for management on a "one share, one vote" basis—back to the late nineteenth century, its public relations campaign to remold the image of corporate control by financiers into one of Jeffersonian democracy did not really begin until the late 1940s.[2]

Until the end of World War II, the public put most of its savings in government bonds because the stock market, which never really recovered from the shock of the Great Depression, still was considered too speculative for small investors. The NYSE, which represented most of the larger corporations in America, thus made the restoration of public confidence in the stock market its main goal in the postwar years.[3]

Before it could easily tap the immense pool of savings in public hands, the NYSE had to instill in potential investors the perception that they had some control over the companies in which they bought shares. "Corporate democracy," by associating the honored participatory mechanisms of democracy with those of stock ownership, served this purpose. "You Make the Financial Weather," began the opening advertisements of the campaign in 1946; "A free market, like a free election, provides a meeting ground for all shades of public opinion and the majority opinion of the moment prevails."[4] "Mass investment," in another advertisement, became "the democratic partner of mass production."[5] Through continued advertising campaigns, press briefings, direct mailings, and speeches and testimony by its officials, as well as the campaigns of its member firms, the NYSE gradually developed the political metaphor to suggest that shareholders, through their votes, controlled American corporations.

Then, in a series of speeches and pamphlets in the early 1950s, mailed to millions of shareholders by the NYSE, G. Keith Funston, the president of the NYSE at that time, pushed the image of "people's capitalism," in which "political freedom makes possible economic democracy." He argued that because all the firms listed on the exchange had to, by NYSE rules, allow shareholders to vote, stock ownership provided "the public with the opportunity to participate directly in corporate affairs." He defined this as "economic democracy"—the immediate forerunner of corporate democracy—and elevated corporate democracy to America's "strongest defense against the foreign isms that would sap our vitality as a nation and turn us over to the evil enemy we know as international communism."

In a speech entitled "America Embraces A People's Capitalism," Funston emphasized the importance of the small shareholder to corporate democracy, noting that voting shareholders—"most of them in the middle and lower income ranges . . ."—have come to hold the vital balance of economic power. Funston argued that this development had greatly benefited the economy, because as corporations grew "more responsive to the general public" through the democratic process, they also became "more creative, more truthful. . .and more fruitful."[6] When he addressed the American Management Association in New York in 1957, he borrowed liberally from the Jeffersonian rhetoric of American politics, stating:

> We believe that if the mass of our people are to risk their dollars on the nation's growth, there is no moral justification in depriving any shareholder in any publicly-held business of a corporate vote.

Funston also enumerated the four basic requisites of corporate democracy:

> First. . .share owners must be assured of a corporate vote; second. . .share owners must be given the machinery and the convenient opportunity to exercise that vote;. . .third, management should be urged to submit for share owner approval the vital proposals affecting a corporation's future;. . .Fourth, because proxy contests for corporate control are a necessary part of the democratic process, the ground rules for fair and honest proxy contests must be further developed and spelled out.

He completed the political analogy with the nostrum that "the burden of making a democratic system work must rest, as it always has, on the . . . nation's share owners."[7] In this analogy, the corporate annual meeting became a quasi-town meeting or, as a president of the NYSE put it in 1972, "the basic forum for shareholder democracy."[8] By the mid-1970s, the practical measure of shareholder democracy became, so far as the NYSE was concerned, the number of customers its member firms had. As a recession set in, it advised, "a decline in share ownership will be viewed as a reversal of the advance of economic democracy."[9] As it turned out, the idea of economic democracy ascended to new heights. By 1986, the NYSE estimated that more than three out of four Americans, either directly or indirectly, owned shares in publicly traded corporations.[10]

By this criterion, the promotion of the democratic metaphor certainly helped alter the public's perception of the extent to which its rights were protected in the stock market. This perception of "corporate democracy" was seen not only as inducing small investors to buy stocks, but also as serving as a prophylactic against government regulation of corporate America. Arthur Levitt, Jr., the chairman of the American Stock Exchange, was called before the Senate Subcommittee on Securities, which was holding hearings on the impact of corporate takeovers in 1985, and asked about the role of corporate democracy. He testified:

> The principle of the central role of the shareholder is widely accepted by the public and by law.... [They] are perceived as the ultimate owners and legitimately the ultimate controllers.[11]

At a time when the rival NYSE was considering abandoning its "one share, one vote" requisite, Levitt went on to warn:

> Corporate executives and directors are wise not to blur that widely endorsed perspective on the primary role of shareholders. Those who would seek to tamper with the present delicate balance between shareholders and directors as their representatives in our corporate governing machinery do so at great ultimate peril.

Levitt explained that the public's perception that there was corporate democracy served to keep government regulators at bay. So long as investors believed there was a democratic process through which they decided major issues, they would see no need for government interference in the area of corporate governance. But, if that perception of corporate democracy was undercut by changes in the heavily touted democratic protections shareholders thought they had, it would lead to demands for "the imposition upon corporate managers of other sorts of accountability." He then asked rhetorically:

> Suppose corporate executives were to come to be perceived by the public as unreachable, as entrenched behind formal barriers beyond the power of a proxy fight or tender offer, and as able to prevent ballot-box expression of views...? Suppose corporate management comes to be perceived as having made themselves accountable to no one?

If those "shifts in public perception" were to occur, Levitt reasoned, there "would likely emerge a more regulated American corporate community built on more restrictive legal controls of business activity." He concluded that the perception of corporate democracy was critical to "our market economy."[12] Whatever its value to the economy, Levitt was on firm ground in arguing that the public perception of corporate democracy had warded off governmental interference. The SEC as well as other regulatory agencies, Congress, and the courts have all cited it as a rationale for nonintervention. The logic here proceeds from the assumption that corporate decisions are made in the final analysis by the elected representatives of the stock owners. As the Supreme Court reasoned in 1977:

> Ultimately, shareholders may decide, through the procedures of corporate democracy, whether their corporation should engage in debate on public issues. Acting through their powers to elect the board of directors or to insist on protective provisions in the corporation's charter, shareholders normally are presumed competent to protect their own interests.[13]

If so, it could scarcely be argued that courts or other government bodies would "be more qualified or entitled to make these kinds of decisions than the shareholders who are the true beneficial owners of the corporation."[14]

What the Senate Subcommittee on Securities failed to ask was, no matter how useful they may be to corporate managers as a prophylactic against regulation, do such public perceptions correspond in any way to reality? Is corporate management, in fact, within the reach of the small shareholders? Can it be displaced under ordinary circumstances by democratic mechanisms such as a "proxy fight" or "ballot-box expressions of views?" Is it accountable to the shareholders through judicial review or any other workable process? Since such store has been placed on the public perception of corporate democracy by officials of the stock exchanges and corporate America, its basic assumptions merit closer inspection.

3 / The Truth About Corporate Democracy: The Fallacy of Electoral Democracy

In its most elemental form, corporate democracy grants the nominal owners of a corporation the right to choose their board of directors in an election supervised by federal law. Except for a few companies which have restricted the voting rights of shareholders through the creation of different—"A" and "B"—classes of stock, including, not without irony, newspaper companies such as The New York Times, The Wall Street Journal, and the Washington Post, most public corporations allow their nominal owners to vote for directors and charter amendments on a "one share, one vote" basis. The idea that each share carries an equal vote is defined by Arthur Levitt as the "cornerstone" of the perception of corporate democracy.

Since they offer the voter no real choice, these elections are "democratic" only in a very limited sense. They are procedurally much more akin to the elections held by the Communist party of North Korea than those held in Western democracies. To begin with, they normally provide only one slate of candidates. In 1985, in well over 99.9 percent of corporate elections, shareholders had to "vote" on a single list of directors chosen by incumbent management. They can, of course, choose not to vote at all, but this offers them little possible chance of having any effect on the result—unless they mount an organized campaign, which is virtually impossible to do without the shareholder list. And management is under no obligation to provide such a list to dissidents. When dissidents have satisfied the disclosure rules of the SEC, management has two choices. It can furnish them a list of stockholders or it can itself mail the dissidents' material to the stockholders. Management usually chooses the latter alternative, which makes it easier to delay the mailing until the last possible moment allowed by SEC regulations. Even if management elects to give the insurgents a list of stockholders, it need not furnish the number of shares held by the stockholders. In this case, dissidents will have to sue under state laws to inspect the stock books (which may require getting written consent from shareholders). Nor is there any secret ballot to protect the identity of any large dissident group, such as pension fund management firms, against reprisals such as depriving them of future contracts to manage pension funds.

Share owners cannot realistically look to the annual meeting as a means of changing management. While their attendance is often encouraged, either live or through closed circuit television, they have no decision-making power. The proxy "vote," which almost always ratifies the unopposed management slate by a wide margin, has already been solicited—and counted—by management. This means that management has in its pocket a sufficient majority of proxies to affirm or deny any measures that may be proposed.

These annual meetings therefore are neither "town meetings" nor "forums" in which the participants decide on issues of community concern, but ceremonial programs, presented by management to inform shareholders of their achievements, projections, and problems. Not uncommonly, there are question and answer periods in which maverick shareholders are permitted to voice their "dissent," but since management is under no obligation to take notice of any suggestions or complaints, they serve little purpose other than to enhance the myth of corporate democracy.

For there to be a competitive election, analogous to those in democratic politics, some stock owner or group of owners must go through the expensive and arduous process of nominating an alternative slate of directors. This is not a minor undertaking, in terms of time, organizational work, or money. The SEC disclosure requirements instituted to foster democratic elections have greatly added to this burden since dissidents are required to submit every conceivable document that bears on their intent, interest, past experience, and associates. They then face the prospect of grueling litigation in which there might be harassing cross-examination on each of the disclosures they made in endless—and expensive—discovery procedures. Typically, the process of having the slate accepted absorbs thousands of hours and costs hundreds of thousands of dollars in legal fees.

That is just the first step. Since there are no primaries or political parties, the challenger must then organize and finance a campaign to solicit proxies from the other share owners to back his slate. To do this, he must obtain the list of share owners. If management does not choose to supply it, he must sue under state law to inspect the corporate records—another expensive and time-consuming process, and one that, under some state laws, requires getting the written consent of other shareholders. After this list is obtained and sifted through for large shareholders, personal contact must be made, which in practice invariably requires the services of an experienced firm of proxy solicitors.

Even at this stage, proxy solicitors are limited in what they can say about incumbent management to what has been "pre-cleared" by the SEC. Under the SEC's proxy rules, insurgents cannot simply say that management is doing a bad job, or that they could do a better one. During the filing and waiting period, they must demonstrably prove, and in advance, that whatever derogatory representations they want to make about management or its performance are accurate—which is difficult at best. Unlike political campaigns, in which charges are freely made, there is no such concept of "freedom of speech" or "freedom of the press" in corporate elections.

The costs of hurdling all the legal barriers and mounting a full-scale proxy battle in a major campaign can run into the millions of dollars. Such a commitment obviously is impossible for most share owners with relatively small holdings. Even if a share owner is willing to spend the money, the chances of winning are extremely slight. Not only does management have the advantage because of its access to corporate information, but it often controls large blocks of voting shares through Employee Stock Option Plan (ESOP) pension plans, trusts, or friendly institutions. It may also stagger election of its directors over three-year periods, so that the dissidents, even if victorious in a given election, do not have control of the board.

In 1984, for example, according to SEC reports, out of some six thousand corporate elections of boards of directors, only eight offered shareholders the possibility of voting for an alternate board of directors, and in only three of these contests did the challenger manage to win control through proxy solicitation. Moreover, even those three were special cases—Management Assistance, Inc., Mutual Real Estate Investment Trust, and Equities Strategies Fund—small companies in which insurgents and their associates owned blocks of stock ranging up to 40 percent.[1] These were exceptions that proved the rule.

Because of the immense costs—and poor odds—involved in waging a proxy battle, virtually all the challenges in 1985 came from investment groups with decisive financial stakes in the challenged company. Small shareholders, who by definition cannot afford the multimillion dollar cost of soliciting proxies or nominating candidates, have no independent means of ensuring a competitive election. A democratic election—which occurs in less than one-tenth of 1 percent of cases—is possible only if a large investor, who can afford the contest, acts as the champion for all the other share owners.

If the idea of corporate democracy is to have any meaning at all, it then must be based on the assumption of indirect participation. The share owners' interests get satisfied not by the dubious power of their votes, it could be argued, but by the ability of large investors, whether institutional or private, in the same company to undertake the expenses of nominating alternative slates of candidates, soliciting proxies, and waging an effective campaign against the incumbents. No matter how self-serving the large investor may be, he will be forced, in this version of corporate democracy, to act as a surrogate for the small investor because his own interest is threatened by the company's mismanagement. The underlying assumption in this view is that what benefits the large investor is what benefits the small investor, and that whatever advantage the large investor gains will also accrue, pro rata, to the small shareholder.

As recent events have amply demonstrated, though, the benefit is both legally and practically divisible. Management is under no obligation—and has no need—to offer small shareholders what it offers a large shareholder to ensure its continued control of the corporation. As court decisions have made crystal clear, management can offer to buy back the shares of a large investor who has acquired sufficient shares to make a challenge feasible without offering the same price to small investors. This corporate practice is called "green mailing" on the notion that management is extorted to pay off the large investor to keep its privileged position (more aptly, it could be called "green skimming," since management uses money taken from share owners, not itself, to gain a benefit).

Commonly, management buys back the potential champion's shares at a premium price in return for a binding agreement that the seller will desist from any further efforts to unseat it. This deal leaves all the other investors with their shares—and no effective means of challenging management (and, adding injury to insult, it almost invariably depresses the value of their investment since the payoff depletes corporate funds). Since 1979, more than $6 billion has been paid out of corporate treasuries for this purpose.[2]

Confronted with this reality, the idea that small share owners can depend on a champion coming to their rescue is nothing short of quixotic. Yet without the possibility of a champion, corporate democracy is left without any real content: the small share owner has no practical means to effect a choice on the corporate ballot.

The Fallacy of Judicial Remedy

Even though share owners lack a practical means to change directors or management, corporate democracy might still be a valid notion if the courts could force boards of directors to act as if the share owners were sovereign. After all, the courts have repeatedly recognized that the shareholders "are the true beneficial owners of the corporation." They further have held that under state law, directors, as the hired representatives of the share owners, have a very definite duty to act in their interests.[3] In addition, corporate charters, which serve as the equivalent of a constitution, grant shareholders certain rights over the disposition of their property. If directors, or the managers they hire, violate these obligations, they can be sued or enjoined by share owners. The threat of court intervention, in this form of corporate democracy, would make management at least accountable to its shareholders.

While this reformulated concept might sound plausible, it assumes that relationships between corporations and their shareholders are governed by uniform law. But this is not the case.

Corporate governance comes mainly under state, not federal, law—except in special circumstances, such as banking or securities regulations. The corporate laws of the states are very different, reflecting different policies as well as different court systems. Most of these state regulations were developed in the nineteenth century, before there was any conflict between owners and managers, and they were designed to give corporate management wide latitude in running their businesses. Confronted by this crazy quilt of state laws, management could choose to incorporate—or reincorporate—in whichever state was most favorable. All it had to do was establish a legal residence, even if only a post office box, and pay a franchise tax. Management, under this system, could choose its own state regulator.

The net effect of this comparative shopping for laws was that smaller states, such as Delaware, Nevada, New Jersey, and Maryland, vied with one another in rewriting their laws to attract corporations as a means of increasing their tax base. The competition between these states, as Justice Louis Brandeis pointed out in 1933, "was not of diligence but of laxity."[4] States competed to write the most favorable laws for corporate management. In this sense, corporate law followed Gresham's Law. State regulations that provided the least opportunity for shareholders to unseat, sue, or harass management tended to displace stricter ones. It soon became, as the late William L. Cary, a former chairman of the SEC, characterized it, a "race for the bottom."[5]

The decisive winner in this race was Delaware, which openly said its policy was to maintain the most "favorable climate" for corporate management.[6] By 1985, Delaware, the second smallest state, had attracted some 166,000 corporations—including most of the Fortune 500 corporations, and 42 percent of all the companies listed on the NYSE.

These absentee corporations paid Delaware over $138 million in franchise taxes in 1985, its largest source of income after personal income taxes.[7] They also provide Delaware corporate lawyers, many of whom go on to be the judges who hear the cases, with most of their legal fees.[8] In addition, Delaware's Chancery Court, which hears most of the major claims against corporate management, has become the paramount arbiter of shareholder rights in America. With other states attempting to emulate this "rent-a-law" success, the accommodative law of Delaware is now, for all practical purposes, the corporate law of the land.

Under this syndrome of state corporate law, it is assumed that shareholders, by virtue of buying stock in a corporation, elect the directors who run it. Further, since they can also appraise the way a corporation is run, shareholders voluntarily accept "the potential risk of bad decisions" that their chosen directors, or the management they hire, might make.[9] Since they freely chose their fate in the hope of making money, shareholders have no right to ask courts to intervene if they misjudge their opportunity. This logic, which has gained the name of the business judgment rule, fortified the court's policy of nonintervention.

Under the business judgment rule, the courts have held that the business decisions of management, no matter how mistaken, unprofitable, or deleterious to the corporation, could not be second-guessed by judges and juries. "The law will not hold directors liable for honest errors . . . even though the errors may be so gross that they may demonstrate the unfitness of the directors to manage the corporate affairs," notes the *Cyclopedia of the Law of Private Corporations*.[10] As stated by the United States Seventh Circuit Court, the rule holds:

> Directors of corporations discharge their fiduciary duties when in good faith they exercise business judgments in making decisions regarding the corporation. . . . In the absence of fraud, bad faith, gross overreaching or abuse of discretions, courts will not interfere with the exercise of business judgment by corporate directors.[11]

In practical terms, this rule provides directors and management with an almost impenetrable shield against shareholders seeking any sort of judicial review of their actions. Under Delaware state law, for share owners to even file a derivative suit against management, they first need to obtain the permission of the board of directors. Where the directors are allied with management, as is almost invariably the case, the dissident shareholders have to demonstrate to the court that permission to sue is being unreasonably withheld. If, however, the issue in question involved a legitimate business decision, the business judgment rule compels the judge to deny the basis for a lawsuit.

While this rule makes considerable sense in shielding directors from lawsuits arising from operational decisions, such as buying equipment or developing new products, it takes on quite a different coloration when applied to their use of corporate assets to retain control of the corporation. There is a critical difference between actions taken by management to run a business on behalf of owners and actions taken to prevent others from replacing them. In recent years, however, the Delaware courts have blurred this distinction by extending the reach of the business judgment rule to cover a wide array of maneuvers used by directors to discourage share owners from challenging them.

These practices, as previously noted, include paying green mail, issuing warrants or debentures that dilute the value of the shares if control is transferred, selling off or optioning highly valued assets to other companies in return for their support of management, creating antitrust conflicts, and deliberately buying valueless properties to make the company less desirable.[12] Despite the fact that such moves are not related to ordinary business objectives, such as enhancing the value of the company, but are aimed at making the shares less desirable to purchase, the Delaware Chancery Court, with some understatement, explained: "not every action taken by a board of directors to thwart a tender offer is to be condemned."[13] The deciding factor was the motive claimed by management, not the result.

To be protected by this expanded business judgment rule, directors need not pick the best course of action, or even be motivated entirely by business considerations. They merely have to claim that there was some business purpose to what they did, even if it was not a good one. The burden of demonstrating that this was untrue, and that there was no conceivable business purpose, was placed on the shareholder. As the Third Circuit said, it must be possible to prove that "impermissible motives predominated in the making of the decision in question."[14] Since "impermissible motive" was defined as one to which no rational business purpose could be attributed, the presumption was not an easy one to overcome. In some circumstances, just remaining in power could be accepted as a rational business purpose under this doctrine. For example, if management sincerely believed, rightly or wrongly, that its removal was not in the best financial interest of the corporation, then its purpose would be deemed permissible.[15]

This interpretation left shareholders little room. The business judgment rule could not be overcome merely by showing that directors were motivated by a desire to perpetuate their own position. It was necessary to demonstrate that the directors' dominant motive was "impermissible." This task is virtually impossible if the directors were coached in what constituted a "rational business purpose" by lawyers well versed in Delaware law.

Consider, for example, the impunity with which the board of directors of Marshall Field & Company in 1977, without the consent or knowledge of shareholders, used corporate funds and misleading information to preserve its own control of what was then the nation's seventh largest retailer. The threat to Marshall Field's incumbent management came from Carter Hawley Hale, another department store chain, in the form of an offer to buy its shares at about twice the market price. Instead of allowing its nominal owners to consider the offer, Marshall Field's management immediately put into effect a defensive strategy, never disclosed to its shareholders, designed to greatly lessen the value of the corporation. The maneuvers involved intentionally depleting its cash reserves by acquiring unprofitable stores—two of which the directors acknowledged in an internal memorandum were "dogs"—and launching new projects in shopping centers in which Carter Hawley Hale had stores for the express purpose of creating antitrust problems. The management of Marshall Field then moved to induce the Department of Justice, Federal Trade Commission, and State of Illinois to commence antitrust investigations—even though they might lead to legal entanglements for itself that could lessen the value of the company.

Management also misled its own shareholders by suggesting that there had been a sudden turnaround in the declining fortunes of the corporation. It reported in late December that its earnings had been up 13 percent for the first nine months of that fiscal year, although it knew from the heavy losses it had already experienced during the all-important Christmas season that for that full year the company actually would lose money (which, as it turned out, amounted to a *25 percent* decline). The result was that share prices temporarily increased, while the underlying assets actually lessened in value. In the face of these defensive moves, Carter Hawley Hale withdrew its offer—and the price of Marshall Field shares dropped by almost 50 percent.

Shareholders, believing that management had misused its prerogatives in initiating these manipulations, thereby violating its fiduciary obligation to them, filed suit against the board of directors in the District Court for the Northern District of Illinois.[16] In an attempt to escape the fatal syndrome of Delaware law, they argued that the manipulations and false disclosures violated the federal securities laws. The court peremptorily dismissed their motion since it found that none of the board of directors' alleged abuses came under federal law, and under Delaware's business judgment rule the board was clearly immune from any liability for such abuses.

On appeal, the United States Court of Appeals not only affirmed the lower court's verdict, but declared that even if the shareholders could unambiguously demonstrate that the directors had purposefully reduced the value of the company to keep control, they could not prevail under Delaware law, and therefore their case could not go to a jury. As for the manipulation of Marshall Field shareholders through the release of misleading information, the court also found federal securities law to be inapplicable.[17]

With no possibility of relief under either federal or state law, the decision left directors in possession of what Judge John Cudahy termed in his partial dissent "an almost irrebuttable presumption of sound business judgment, prevailing over everything but the elusive hobgoblins of fraud, bad faith, or abuse of discretion." He noted: "Unfortunately, the majority here has moved one giant step closer to shredding whatever constraints still remain on the ability of corporate directors to place self-interest above shareholder interest. . . ."[18]

Even before this "giant step," shareholder suits hardly could be considered effective deterrents to corporate management's acting contrary to shareholder interests. To even bring a suit against some or all of the directors on behalf of the corporation, shareholders under state law need to seek the permission of the directors. If that is not forthcoming, they can then ask the court to excuse them from this requisite. If, however, the directors are shielded by the business judgment rule, the shareholders can be denied the right to proceed with the suit. In any case, only shareholders with large stakes in the corporation are usually in a position to afford such a lengthy undertaking (and such shareholders can be bought out through a green mail settlement).

Under such circumstances, it is not surprising that few such suits ever get off the ground. Professor Stuart R. Cohn, analyzing this problem in the *Texas Law Review* in 1984, found only seven shareholder suits, which did not involve fraud, that were successful. He concluded that "cases that assess damages against negligent management are rare to the point of becoming an endangered species."[19]

The ultimate rationalization for judicial nonintervention in business decisions is the assumption by the courts that intervention is unnecessary because management, through the board of directors, must answer directly to shareholders for any mistakes it makes. In the Marshall Field ruling, for example, the United States Court of Appeals simply stated as a "fact" the proposition that "the director wants to enhance corporate profits to keep shareholders satisfied so that they won't oust him."[20] This reasoning presents a catch-22 situation: the legal system, assuming shareholders have the elective power to oust directors, provides directors with a virtually impregnable shield (the business judgment rule) that enables them to use corporate assets to make their removal all but impossible. The very presumption by the courts that there is some form of corporate democracy deprives the shareholders of the means of achieving it. This may be true even when dissident shareholders control a majority of the voting stock, as the Hi-Shear case demonstrates.

The board of directors of Hi-Shear, a successful California technology company, was challenged in 1974 by a single dissident shareholder by the name of Frank Klaus, who had acquired 50 percent of the voting stock. The directors responded by issuing a large number of new shares— amounting to about 20 percent of the shares outstanding—which it put into friendly hands. Half were sold at a bargain price to two small companies that, in turn, agreed to vote them in support of the board; the rest were donated to Hi-Shear's own Employee Stock Ownership Trust (ESOT). These new shares sufficiently diluted the dissident's holdings to defeat the challenge. Klaus's only redress was to sue the board of directors on the grounds that its purpose in issuing the stock was not ordinary business but overriding the will of the majority to preserve its own control. While the California court* ruled that even though Klaus had demonstrated that a "substantial purpose" of the board of directors in diluting the stock was keeping control, the board still was shielded by the business judgment rule on the ground that it also had a business purpose in distributing the shares to the other companies.[21]

To be sure, courts have recognized outer limits on how far management can go in negating the voting rights of its share owners. In a recent case tried under New York law, in which a challenged board of directors transferred a controlling block of voting shares to a Panamanian subsidiary and its ESOP management, the court found that, under the state's business judgment rule, this manipulation constituted self-dealing. Consequently, it enjoined management from voting the shares for itself. (The court was able to apply New York law in this instance because the subsidiary was registered in Panama, not Delaware.[22])

The courts have also drawn the line at management transferring to itself, without the approval of share owners, control of the key assets

---

* The California court did look askance at the blatant use of management-controlled ESOTs to perpetuate control, but this was another issue.

of the corporation. For example, when Revlon's management attempted to retain control by giving a highly dubious option for corporation assets to a favorite group in which it once had an equity interest, even the Delaware Chancery Court recognized that the appearance of self-dealing overrode the protection of the business judgment rule.[23] The court here, while denying one egregious tactic, at the same time affirmed the board's broader strategy of using corporate assets to retain power, noting:

> . . . the directors have the right, even the duty, to adopt defensive measures to defeat a takeover attempt which is perceived as being contrary to the best interests of the corporation and its shareholders.[24]

In other words, so long as directors perceive that their removal would somehow not best serve the corporate interest, they can do anything to stay in power short of naked self-dealing.

Finally, courts have been willing to intervene if it can be demonstrated that directors have recklessly disregarded their obligation to act with due diligence in accomplishing their objective—or go through the motions. In the odd case of *Transunion Corporation,* where the directors demonstrably acted in unnecessary haste and sloppiness in selling the company before considering relevant information about other bids, the Delaware Chancery Court held that the directors were liable for damages to the shareholders. It made it clear, though, that the directors' exposure came not from the substance of their decision to sell the company but from their negligence in not following the prescribed process.[25] In affirming the right of a board of directors to do what it wished with a company, so long as it does it in the prescribed manner, the court sent the message to management and its legal advisers that the appearance of due diligence was what mattered. Consequently, to make themselves invulnerable to this sort of liability, boards of directors had to follow a checklist of procedures prescribed by their counsel.[26]

Delaware court-watchers interpreted this new concern with form as little more than a public relations ploy, meant to redress press reports suggesting that the Delaware courts had been too lenient on management in previous decisions. In any case, the effect of this verdict was not to make it any easier to unseat management—since law firms were perfectly capable of coaching directors on what constituted the correct form of deliberation—but to increase the cost of liability insurance for directors.[27] In June 1986, Delaware partially remedied this situation by enacting a law that allowed corporations, with the approval of their shareholders, to limit this liability.[28]

Though it has not yet reached the absolute bottom, the corporate race toward the least restrictive laws has gone sufficiently far to leave shareholders with no realistic possibility that courts could either enforce their rights as owners when they wish to change or remove directors—or the managers who are often in league with them. As the law now stands, shareholders cannot depend on either state or federal law to even allow them to bring suit to stop directors and managers from entrenching themselves in office, and at their expense, by "restructuring" the entity. Nor can federal regulatory agencies be asked to intervene in anything other than violations of the securities laws. While the courts and SEC pay homage to the idea of "corporate democracy," they do not provide the shareholders with the means to bring it about.

The Fallacy of the Free Market Theory

Once the veneer of democratic processes is stripped away, the shareholder has only one remedy available if he disagrees with the stewardship of his corporation. He can sell his stock. This final option has led some theorists to recast corporate democracy in an economic, rather than political, metaphor. Professor Henry G. Manne, the director of the Law and Economic Center at Emory University, for example, suggests that even without any proxy contests, disclosure rules, shareholder meetings, or judicial review, "an enormous amount of power and control is exercised by the owners of the business, albeit not in...a political fashion."[29]

The way that a shareholder effectively "votes," according to Manne, is by selling his shares to the highest bidder. As he sees it, shareholders are fully informed of the financial health of a company, not by SEC disclosure forms, but by the market price of the stock—which is all that counts if it is assumed that all relevant information in an efficient market is subsumed in that price. Given this theory, the power to sell shares carries weight, as far as management is concerned, because selling off shares can lower the value of the corporation in the marketplace. Thus, to prevent a widespread exodus from the company by shareholders, and a lowering of the share price, management has no choice but to attempt to placate shareholders by doing what they want. But this economic theory requires more than a shareholder being free to sell his holdings to another investor. Merely selling shares is analogous to political refugees leaving a dictatorship by "voting with their feet." While it may solve their personal problem, it does not end, or necessarily even weaken, the dictatorship—though it might weaken the economy. Similarly, just the exchange of one powerless shareholder for another in a corporation, while it may lessen the market price of shares, will not dislodge management—or even threaten it. On the contrary, if dissident shareholders leave, it may even bring about the further entrenchment of management—especially if management can pass new bylaws in the interim.

This theory works if, and only if, shareholders can sell their shares eventually to an investor who has the power to take over the company—and fire the ruling board of directors. The lurking corporate raider, who is ready and able to combat management when he receives even a "signal" of shareholder discontent, is the critical figure here. The scenario, according to Manne, goes as follows: "As shareholders sell shares over and over, they force the share price to go down...signal[ing] to the world, including potential raiders, that something is wrong with the management of the company." Because management has no defense against raiders taking control, it is ultimately pressured by share selling "to behave in the interest of owners."[30]

In this unrestricted "corporate control market," as Manne defines it, the price of shares at any given moment includes the assets value and the right to take control. Therefore, all a raider requires to take over a corporation is for the price of control to fall low enough, compared to the asset value, to warrant his intervention.[31] The underlying premise in this ingenious theory is that there actually exists a free market for corporate control.

In fact, this market for corporate control had been historically anything but free. For one thing, taking control of any company which competed in the same markets was restricted by both state and federal antitrust laws, and takeovers in many industries, including banking, insurance companies, utilities, and broadcasting, required governmental approval. For another, unfriendly takeovers, aimed at unseating management, were a rare phenomenon up until the end of the 1970s. In the past, large corporations tended to shy away from entangling themselves in antitrust and other debilitating regulatory battles, as well as what were almost certain to be grueling counterattacks from the besieged management. Individuals, except in a few extraordinary cases, were unable to obtain the necessary bank financing for a major takeover. There were mergers, of course, but these were for the most part alliances between friendly managements. By combining with other companies into "conglomerates," management not only increased its resources, but it made itself less vulnerable to being taken over: any potential acquirer would have to reckon with the antitrust implications since the mergers usually increased the number of areas in which a corporation was engaged. Mergers also further disbursed stock ownership by increasing the number of shareholders. In this sense, such mergers further limited the scope of any real market for corporate control.

To be sure, not all of these intercorporate mergers and acquisitions could be characterized as friendly. Some managements bitterly resisted becoming part of a conglomerate. But they usually did so by appealing either to state regulatory authorities—as Mead did in its battle against Occidental Petroleum—thereby entangling those seeking to take over the corporation in potentially embarrassing public disclosures, or by simply disposing of the specific parts of the company needed for the combination to be advantageous. They were thus able to rely on outer defenses to discourage bidders.

But the real test of the free market in corporate control came with the rise of individual "takeover entrepreneurs," backed by the innovative financing of Drexel Burnham. Conventional defenses, designed to ward off conglomerates, did not work effectively against them. Raiders such as T. Boone Pickens, Ronald Perlman, Carl Icahn, and Sir James Goldsmith had virtually no exposure to state or federal antitrust laws, since the corporate shells they set up for the takeovers did not compete with their targets. Nor, as individuals, were they vulnerable to counterattack by their own shareholders or by public relations campaigns. They were in the business of one-time takeovers, and not interested in maintaining any particular corporate image. Since they did not necessarily seek any particular divisions of the targeted companies for any kind of "synergy," they also could not be discouraged by the sale of any unit—so long as they could realize a profit from the remainder of the company. Once they demonstrated that they had the ability to marshal billions of dollars in commitments, though not cash, they could openly bid for control of corporations. This development in the 1980s, as well as the Court's striking down of anti-takeover laws, threatened to create for the first time a really open market in corporate control.

Not surprisingly, this sort of free market was not readily accepted by corporate America. Far from allowing share owners to "vote" by selling control to the raiders, most, if not all, of the established corporate managers that were challenged moved to block this threat by erecting whatever barriers they could to control being transferred. If legal means to do so were not available to them in the state in which they resided, they often reincorporated in states with more favorable laws. If their corporate charters prevented them from denying share owners the right to freely sell control to outsiders, the managers proposed changes and amendments. If some shareholders refused to vote their proxies for this curtailment of their rights—as did a number of large institutional investors, such as the State of California Pension Funds—management, with the assistance of ingenious outside law firms, notably Wachtell Lipton, invented devices, not requiring share owner approval, that made it extremely difficult (and expensive) for their shareholders to tender their stock to the challenger.

They did so, they argued, because their share owners did not have the information, or necessary vision of the future, to make a choice for themselves. They also held that share owners, by not entrusting such decisions to management, which had the necessary data for making these decisions, would be likely to adversely affect the rights of others, such as their employees, suppliers, and the communities in which they were located. Whatever the validity of these claims, they served to deny the legitimacy of a market in corporate control—or, at least, of owners freely participating in it.[32]

To win support for this position, a long roster of chief executive officers of multibillion dollar corporations presented the sort of arguments in front of congressional committees that were usually made by public or quasi-public officials: the managers were calling for government intervention in the marketplace to stop hostile takeovers.

For example, in hearings before the Senate Subcommittee on Banking in June 1985, Fred L. Hartley, the rough-talking chairman of Unocal Corporation, testified about the offer made to buy his company at almost twice the market price by T. Boone Pickens earlier that year. Hartley considered Pickens's attempt a form of subversive and pernicious activity. He called on Congress to "destroy the financial barbarians" behind such hostile takeovers, and he specifically proposed that it legislate a moratorium on all further "hostile takeovers."

In explaining his position, Hartley said that he would permit "mergers," which he considered salutary, but not "hostile" raids, which he considered destructive; the sole distinction between the two being that the former were approved by management, and the latter were not. According to this definition, the proposed moratorium would preclude transfers of corporate control without the approval of management. This brought a heated reply by Sir James Goldsmith. He responded:

> I'd like to analyze that word. Hostile to who? Hostile to the entrenched management, not hostile to the shareholders. Who's calling it hostile? The owners of the business?...It's only hostile because those who mistakenly come to believe that they own the business...don't want to give it up.

He then went on to suggest that there was a double standard:

> There is no difference between a raid and a merger except that an established bureaucrat loses his job [in the former]. This whole game has been changed to bring in buzz words which are deformed. The word hostile is merely a bureaucratic term to try and create a nobility to entrenchment.[33]

Though Goldsmith dismissed this difference between "mergers" and "raids" as irrelevant to the issue, the possibility that managers would be thrown out of concerns to which they had dedicated their careers was of great concern to established corporations. The Business Roundtable, which represents (and lobbies for) the views of most of the nation's larger corporations, warned that continued hostile takeovers could catastrophically damage the structure of American business.[34] In this atmosphere, nearly half the Fortune 500 companies changed their charters or bylaws to lessen the possibility that shareholders could dislodge management through the elective machinery. In some cases, rather than a majority of 50 percent of the votes, corporations amended their charters to require a "supermajority" of 75 percent of the votes to oust the board of directors. Thus, so long as a board could count on the support of only 25 percent of the votes, through its relations with pension funds, stock trusts, or institutional investments, it had what amounted to permanent tenure in office.

Corporations also instituted "classified boards," thus staggering the directors' terms over three years. This meant that even if a raider bought the majority of the stock in a company, he could elect only one-third of the directors in the first year. Since under Delaware law, share owners cannot remove directors until their terms expire—except for "cause," which requires a trial—control of the acquired company would remain in the hands of directors that could not be replaced for at least two years; only then could the raider elect a majority of the directors of the company he now owned.

In addition, to further immunize themselves against a sustained challenge, corporate boards obtained from shareholders the discretionary right to issue so-called blank-check shares of preferred stock, which had multiple voting rights. Typically, these blank-check shares would carry the voting weight of one ordinary share. With such a device in place, even if a raider acquired enough shares of the ordinary stock to give him a supermajority of the votes, the board could dilute his voting rights by distributing the blank-check shares to its supporters. For example, when the board of Carter Hawley Hale was challenged for control by The Limited, Inc., it issued its blank-check voting shares to a third company, General Cinema, which agreed to vote them decisively in its support.[35]

Carrying these changes to their logical end, an increasing number of corporations sought to reverse the "one share, one vote" principle, which had been cited as the cornerstone of corporate democracy. In some of these "dual classification" plans, the stock would be divided into two classes of shares: "A" and "B" stock. The "A" shares would have sufficient voting rights to assure it elected the directors, while the "B" shares would share in the profit. Other plans have based voting rights on the length of time shares were owned.[36] While the ability to implement such plans for companies listed on the NYSE had been inhibited up until recently by the threat of suspension from the exchange, in July 1986 the NYSE changed its policy, allowing companies to issue "dual classes" of stock.

The changes sought by management require the approval of the shareholders. Although institutional investors, which now hold a large portion of the common shares in these corporations, have tended to oppose some of these defenses against takeovers, especially supermajority requirements and classified boards, management, with the support of friendly banks and controlled ESOP plans, frequently managed to solicit sufficient proxies to enact these defensive amendments in shareholder meetings. In 1985, for example, of 408 corporate proposals intended to restrict contests for control, only 19 were voted down.[37] Management is assisted at times in passing these amendments by pension funds that, after selling their blocks, still want to curry favor with management to enhance their future business prospects. Since they remain, up to a prescribed time, the shareholder of record, they can still vote for management's amendments.[38] After Goldsmith purchased large blocks of shares in Crown Zellerbach in March and April 1985, he found that the pension funds that sold them to him (but remained nominal owners until May) voted in favor of all the anti-takeover devices that management proposed.[39]

Moreover, once these anti-takeover changes are enacted, even though the circumstances might change, they do not have to be voted on again by future shareholders. In terms of the number of corporations passing "defensive" resolutions, this "anti-raider" campaign proved extraordinarily effective.

The anti-raider campaign was also used to justify management awarding itself hundreds of millions of dollars in termination agreements called "golden parachutes." These payments were originally conditioned on management not quitting if ownership changed hands, and, as an incentive for preserving the management team under unsettled conditions, they served a legitimate business purpose. They were modified by management, however, to allow it to quit at its own discretion, and still get the huge severance payments. It thus presented another costly barrier to raiders. Not only would managers have a strong cash incentive to quit, but if they did they would take with them a substantial share of the corporation's cash. The managers of Revlon, a cosmetics company, for example, received over $80 million in compensation after a takeover, which was about 5 percent of the value of the company on the stock market. One set of shareholders might enact a supermajority amendment, requiring 80 percent of shareholders to alter anti-takeover defenses, and future shareholders would have to abide by it.

4 / The Poison Pill

Under the pressure of potential takeovers, corporate management also took decisive measures to end challenges to its control that did not require the approval of shareholders. The main justification given shareholders for these peremptory defenses was that corporate raiders used unfair tactics in making their tender offers—specifically, the "two-tier tender offer." There was at least some element of truth in this charge.

In the two-tier offer, raiders first tendered for only the number of shares sufficient to give them control—usually 51 percent. The raiders then agreed, after control of the company was assured, to buy the balance of the shares at a lower price. In many of these deals, the first "tier" was a cash offer, while the second "tier" was for unrated corporate debentures, worth only a fraction of the price or cash offered for the shares already tendered.

The quandary posed by the two-tier tender offer was akin to the so-called Prisoner's Dilemma, the situation that arises when two friends are arrested as suspects in a crime and, unable to communicate with each other, are offered a deal. One of the suspects is told that if he informs on his friend he will go free, but that if he does not, and his friend informs on him, he will go to prison. Whereas it would be in the best interest of both to remain silent, since they would then both go free, each is compelled to inform on the other by his concern that if he does not talk he will be informed on by the other.

In the case of a two-tier offer, shareholders have to take similar precautions. No matter how much they oppose the deal, if they refuse to submit their shares—the equivalent of remaining silent—and other shareholders do, they will lose their right to participate in the first tier at a premium. If other shareholders do submit their shares, and the raider gains control of the company, they would be forced then to take the lower price offered in the second tier. If, on the other hand, they tender, they at least participate pro rata in the higher offer. (If the raider fails to win control, in either case, the deal is off, and nothing is lost.) The two-tier deal was thus one that could not be prudently turned down.

In attempting to remedy this kind of coercion and restore, as he put it, "a level playing field," Martin Lipton, the senior partner in the New York law firm of Wachtell Lipton, developed a defensive device which became known as the "poison pill." It was derived from a standard feature in ordinary convertible bonds, called the "flip-over" provision. Because purchasers of convertible bonds had the right to convert the bond into a set number of shares in the company, they had to be given protection if the company was acquired or merged into another company. To guard against this contingency, bondholders usually were given the right to convert their bonds into the stock of the acquiring company at a fixed ratio based equitably on the difference between the share prices of the two companies. Any company that took over and merged with another company that had such flip-over convertible bonds outstanding had to abide by the provisions in them, just as it assumed the debts of the company.

In creating the poison pill, Wachtell Lipton merely changed the conversion ratio in the flip-over provision so that rather than being just fair to the bondholder in the event the company was acquired, it would provide him with a windfall profit. Usually, the ratio was adjusted to two to one, which gave the holder the right to buy shares in the acquiring company worth $100 for $50. The idea behind this provision was not to unduly benefit the bondholder, but make it ruinously costly for the acquiring company.

While Wachtell Lipton custom designed many variations on this theme, such as convertible flip-over preferred shares, the central mechanism of the poison pill remained the same: Under specified circumstances, such as an outsider making a tender offer not approved by the board or buying a certain percentage of the stock, a "right" would be activated to all current shareholders. This "right," which could be sold or traded separate from the stock, typically allowed the holder of it to buy a poison pill bond for $50 that could be flipped over into $100 worth of stock of any company that acquired it and then merged with it. Once activated, like the doomsday machine in the film *Dr. Strangelove,* the poison pill cannot be revoked—even by the board of directors. If the raider then proceeds with the takeover, shareholders can use their rights to buy, through the device of the convertible right, shares in the raider's company at a small fraction of their market price. Since no company could allow this dilution to occur, corporations that swallow the poison pill become "unmergeable."

However benign its original intent, the poison pill became in short order a powerful potion against takeovers. By 1985, over ninety corporations had adopted some version of the poison pill.[1] The deterrent effect of the flip-over provision was usually sufficient so that the "rights" did not have to be distributed to shareholders. In only one instance where the rights were activated was a company taken over.

This singular exception, Crown Zellerbach, is instructive. The management of Crown Zellerbach, a San Francisco-based conglomerate, had adopted a poison pill that took effect if any outsider acquired 20 percent or more of its shares without the approval of its board. In 1985, after the board rejected an offer made by Sir James Goldsmith to buy the entire company, he bought slightly over 20 percent of its shares, thereby activating the pill. Even though the flip-over provision made it infeasible to merge Crown Zellerbach into his—or any other—company, Goldsmith continued buying shares in the open market until he had acquired control of the conglomerate. Then, through a convoluted and extremely expensive process aimed at bypassing the poison pill, he allowed shareholders in Crown Zellerbach to swap their stock for stock in different divisions of the conglomerate. After this dismembering, what remained of Crown Zellerbach was sold to another company, James River, which operated it as an unconsolidated subsidiary. Technically, it was therefore still a separate company, which meant that there was no acquiring company into which the lethal rights could be flipped over.

The loophole through which Goldsmith got around the poison pill, however, was blocked by a new version of the poison pill. This new defense added a "flip-in" provision to the conventional poison pill that allowed the holders of the units to convert them either into shares of the acquiring company or into shares in their own company at a bargain price. Any raider who acquired his shares after the poison pill rights were distributed thus faced the prospect of having the shares he had bought in the company diluted by these newly issued shares. Whereas the flip-over pill could be evaded, as Goldsmith did, by gaining control but not actually merging the acquired company, the flip-in pill made it all but impossible for raiders to gain effective control: Their purchases over a fixed percent would trigger the issuance of new stock to everyone else at a cheaper price.

This version of the poison pill gave management a means of withdrawing its company from any free market in corporate control—without the approval of shareholders. Although proponents of the pill, including Lipton, have taken the position, in public hearings, that the poison pill is only designed to stop abusive, non-cash tender offers by forcing raiders to negotiate directly with boards of directors, courts have not so restricted their usage.[2] As Lipton himself pointed out in a letter to his clients on October 24, 1985, "On the bright side, the Court specifically approved our Note Purchase Rights Plan ("Poison Pill")....The Court seems to say that a company with a rights plan may decide to reject any takeover bid—even an all and any case offer."[3]

Even corporations that did not have a poison pill in place at the time of a challenge could adopt ad hoc defenses that made takeovers infeasible. When, in 1985, Fred Hartley and the Unocal board of directors were challenged for control by T. Boone Pickens, they adopted the so-called lollipop defense in which they offered to buy shares at a premium of about 50 percent from everyone but Pickens and his group. This redemption cost some $4 billion, which required mortgaging a good part of Unocal's asset value. The Pickens group—Pickens and his associates comprised the largest group of shareholders in Unocal—were arbitrarily excluded from this offer, but they would be saddled with the debt. This lollipop maneuver was analogous to a building manager borrowing heavily on the property from a bank, and giving the proceeds to one partner in league with him, while leaving the other partners with the burden of repaying the debt.

Confronted with this potential financial disaster, Pickens and his associates had to abandon their challenge. Hartley then offered to buy back a portion of their shares at a premium price in return for their agreeing not to attempt future raids to oust management.[4] Despite the deference he paid to shareholder rights in his Senate testimony, Hartley had, when it came to the matter of control of his own company, negated the bedrock principle of fairness in the stock market—the principle that all share owners should share equally, proportionate to their holdings, in any distribution of corporate benefits. (Indeed, the only limit the Delaware court put on defensive measures was to insist that once a board elects to sell the company, as was, for example, the case with Revlon, it must hold a fair auction and not exclude any bidders.)

When the Delaware Supreme Court upheld the right of directors under siege to exclude whatever dissident shareholders they chose from corporate benefits, and affirmed the poison pill in November 1985, it effectively ended the idea of a free market in corporate control. With defenses as potent as the flip-in poison pill and the lollipop against all hostile offers—cash as well as two-tier bond offers—corporate management, regardless of whether stockholders sold their shares to raiders, could still retain control by diluting the value of its shares. They went well beyond creating a "level playing field"; they turned the market for corporate control into a dangerous mine field for anyone challenging management.

By the end of September 1986, with over 300 major corporations having some variant of the poison pill defense in place, hostile takeovers had become a rare phenomenon. In the first nine months of the year, there had been only one successful hostile takeover, NL Industries, and this single success proceeded from an interpretation of the New Jersey law governing poison pills that would not apply to corporations incorporated outside of New Jersey. Even if this decision were sustained in invalidating the poison pill in New Jersey, it would only induce directors to reincorporate in Delaware or other permissive states to evade any threat of their defenses being breached.

To end even the possibility of the loss of control through a competitive auction, corporate management has been lobbying state legislatures in New York, New Jersey, Idaho, Minnesota, Kentucky, and California to pass laws prohibiting any takeovers that were not approved by corporate boards of directors. The New Jersey bill, which is currently being considered by its senate, would require anyone acquiring 10 percent or more of stock in a New Jersey-based company, or any company that does more than 10 percent of its business in that state, to get the permission of its board if he wanted to effect a merger or liquidation within five years. Until that approval is obtained, he could not increase his holdings past 10 percent without suffering this penalty. Such shield laws mean that managers, as long as they remained allied with their directors (whom they appoint), can keep their jobs whatever shareholders decide to do with their stock.[5] As more states pass laws making it impossible for "hostile" share owners to dispossess their managers, or upset what legislators have taken to call the "corporate community," management will be placed, in law as well as fact, beyond the reach of some idealized auction for corporate control.

The idea of a free market in corporate control, though appealing theoretically, turns out to be inconsistent with reality. Management has sufficient power, buttressed by state law and the recent decisions of the Delaware court, to either snuff out almost any challenges from dissidents or make them prohibitively expensive to pursue. The very existence of such power fatally flaws the economic reformulation of corporate democracy. In any form, political or economic, share owners simply do not have the means available to them, either directly or through surrogates, to compel their managers to act in the shareholders' interests. The last nail was driven into the long-sealed coffin of corporate democracy in July 1986 by the NYSE when it abandoned its prohibition against listed corporations issuing different classes of stock with different voting rights, effectively putting to rest the principle of "one share, one vote."

Why Not a Free Market in Corporate Control?

Corporate America's arguments against allowing any free market in corporate control were based not on considerations about the rights of shareholders or, for that matter, the free market, but on pragmatic claims about the effect of takeovers on the American economy. They held that hostile takeovers had "externalities" for others in the community. Nicholas F. Brady, the chairman of Dillon Read & Company—the investment bank that represented Unocal in its fight against Pickens—writing in *The New York Times* raised the specter of the "crash of 1929" after asserting: "The takeover frenzy perils the economy." Specifically, they foresaw three disastrous consequences:

1. Since such takeovers were often predicated on "busting up" the target and selling off assets to pay for the cost of its acquisition, they warned that takeovers would lead to the shutdown of vital businesses and massive unemployment. In his testimony, Hartley suggested that if Unocal had been taken over by outsiders, it might "go down the tube and there would be 22,000 people out of work," adding "we're trying to defend this country...from having that happen."[6]

2. Since corporate raiders usually had to finance their acquisitions by borrowing on the bond market, it was argued that their continued activities would permanently burden corporations with an economically unjustifiable load of debt. Felix Rohatyn, a senior partner in Lazard Freres & Company, an investment bank that was advising many corporations on their defenses, wrote in the *Wall Street Journal*: "Under the banner of deregulation and total faith in the marketplace, we're impairing our greatest of assets: the credibility of our capital markets and the faith in our financial institutions."[7] He also warned in testimony before the Senate Subcommittee on Banking that the financing of takeovers could result in a catastrophic collapse of overextended financial institutions. He explained: "This activity weakens many of our companies by stripping away their equity and replacing it with high-cost debt."[8]

3. Since corporations with lower earnings tend to be more vulnerable, it is argued that the threat of a takeover forces corporate management to favor near-term over far-term earnings. Lipton testified on this point: "The situation can be analogized to a farmer who does not rotate his

crops, does not periodically let his land lie fallow and does not protect his land...In the early years he will maximize his return from the land...but inevitably it leads to a dust bowl and economic disaster."[9]

While these dramatic assertions may have heightened public fears about the effects of takeovers, they had little basis in empirical reality. Although corporations often use the imagery of "institutions" in describing their service, they are private combinations of capital and skills organized for the purpose of producing profits. As such, they routinely lay off workers when orders decline, close down or relocate factories when it is advantageous to do so, and change suppliers when they get a better deal.

Corporate raiders aim for these same economies. When they effect a so-called bust-up takeover, they do not actually close down productive divisions of the business they acquire; they sell them to whichever corporate management values them the most. Their profit depends on finding corporations that can make better use of the assets than the company that has been taken over. As it turns out, between 1980 and 1986, the raiders succeeded in taking over only a handful of companies—including Diamond International, Continental Group, Revlon, SCM, AMF, Crown Zellerbach, Datapoint, and TWA—and, in all cases, these bust ups involved the sale of divisions to companies that continued operating them. In some cases, these enforced reorganizations increased the total employment of the divisions that were sold. In the breakup of Diamond International, for example, all its divisions except for its timber holdings were sold to other companies over a five-year period. In every case these businesses were expanded by the management that acquired them, resulting in increased employment. Goldsmith, who accomplished this bust-up takeover, observed in his testimony before the Subcommittee: "Each one of these companies liberated from the dead hand of a tired conglomerate has prospered."[10] In other cases, such as Datapoint, the reorganizations no doubt led to consolidations, and some loss of jobs. In these latter instances, even if ownership had not changed hands, however, any new management seeking higher productivity could also have eliminated redundant jobs. The balancing of efficiency against unemployment is a legitimate but independent issue.

Takeovers, moreover, do not inevitably saddle corporations with unmanageable debt. This misunderstanding proceeds from the assumption that debt, once incurred, cannot be removed. Debt, however, is not permanent. Even though corporations may have to borrow temporarily for takeover activities, they need not maintain the debt if it becomes burdensome. There is a huge, readily available market in corporate debt, exceeding $200 billion, in which investment banking houses such as

Salomon Brothers, Drexel Burnham, and Morgan Stanley specialize in swapping corporate debt for equity (and vice versa). A corporation that prefers to lessen its debt can issue new shares and swap them for its outstanding bonds, which it can then retire. This is true not only of high-grade bonds (those rated AA or higher), but also of the so-called junk bonds (those rated BB+ or less). The market in these bonds alone is between $75 and $100 billion.[11] In point of fact, such recapitalizations happen every day. Through such decisions, corporate treasurers elect their debt to equity ratio, presumably on the basis of the comparative costs of the different financial instruments.

Although takeovers have resulted in increased corporate debt, as critics have noted, most of that debt is the result of friendly acquisitions and mergers—not raids. Consider R. J. Reynolds's "friendly" purchase of Nabisco for $4.5 billion in 1985—the largest non-oil takeover in history. The arrangement was a two-tiered tender offer that involved the issuance of massive corporate debt. The lack of criticism of the leveraging that proceeded from friendly takeovers or leveraged buyouts by management raised some question about the sincerity of the concern. As Goldsmith pointed out in the hearings: "The only difference is the Nabisco management has been reassured as to its future tenancy in the management structure." In any case, if the ratio of corporate debt to equity gets out of hand, the government and federal reserve systems have means of remedying it that do not require ending the market for corporate control.

Similarly, the hypothesis that concern over hostile takeovers forces managers, like foolish dirt farmers, to neglect the future of their enterprises to maximize current earnings is based on a fallacy. It incorrectly assumes that the stock market price of a company is based solely on its current earnings. But share prices are based on estimated future streams of earnings as well as present earnings. This is, of course, why stocks have very different price-to-earnings ratios. Companies that are perceived to have more promising futures, such as biotechnology companies, have high prices relative to their earnings; conversely, companies perceived to have bleak futures, such as depleting oil companies, have a low price relative to their earnings. Management therefore cannot really hope to raise the share price by neglecting future development.

Nor is there any evidence that the threat of takeovers results in a reduction of R&D expenses by targeted corporations. A study conducted by the SEC's Office of Chief Economist in 1985 examined 217 firms that were acquisition targets between 1981 and 1984. It showed that R&D expenditures had been only half the average of other firms up until the time of the takeover threat, and that afterward there was no appreciable change in these expenditures.[12]

What is at stake is not the economic utility of hostile takeovers, but the consequences of further restricting, or even eliminating entirely, the market in corporate control. By raising the economic chimeras of mass unemployment, financial collapse, and a corporate "dust bowl," corporate management has succeeded not only in diverting attention from this issue but also in providing rationales for the erection of further barriers to any challenges to its own control.

5 / The Future of Ownerless Capitalism: A Worst-Case Scenario

Without any real mechanism to assure corporate democracy or transfer control, the continued dispersion of ownership, through stock splits and new issues, will gradually lead to the transfer of control over most of America's productive capital from its legal owners to the hands of management groups. Moreover, since these groups will be self-perpetuating, appointing themselves and their allies to boards of directors, they need not be accountable to anyone in the management of these assets. Eventually, this will result in a complete separation of ownership from management—the culmination of a phenomenon that began early this century. This development cannot help but affect the way American capitalism works—as opposed to how it is supposed to work.

To begin with, management, freed of the demands made by owners to maximize their return on capital, would have no compelling motive to reinvest earnings in the most efficient way (or return them, in the form of dividends, to the owners). Its rational incentive instead would be to maximize the benefits it derives from the corporation, which would include more than direct compensation. Executives in control could, like Armand Hammer, the chairman of Occidental Petroleum, legally use corporate revenue to buy art, sponsor peace festivals, build international trade centers in Communist countries, make political contributions, and have private airliners at their disposal. They would not have to maximize earnings but only produce the minimum necessary to maintain the company.

Moreover, if corporate management cannot be held responsible by owners for meeting any unambiguous measures of performance, such as sales, profits, or growth, it would operate under no different constraints from those on the management of other large bureaucratic organizations, such as government agencies. In such bureaucratic enterprises, the goal characteristically becomes the perpetuation of the organization itself rather than any external objective. Entrenched executives, who view themselves as custodians of institutions rather than managers of businesses, can be expected to put a higher value on maintaining peaceful relations with labor unions, suppliers, community representatives, and competitors than increasing the market share through new products or lower prices. While such actions may create less conflict, they would also create dislocation in supply and demand, and stagnation. Under these circumstances, ownerless capitalism would produce an economy that depended on managerial bureaucracies, intent on preserving themselves, to allocate the nation's resources. It would be, in effect, socialism without any social responsibility.

If it becomes readily apparent that the mechanisms of corporate democracy are wholly fictitious, the rationale for the state and federal government not intervening in the private sphere will evaporate. Arthur Levitt, Jr., the head of the American Stock Exchange, pointed out that without the presumption that corporate managers are accountable to their owners, there would be no logical barrier to governments passing laws regulating business. As the concept of "private capital" becomes increasingly blurred, the distinction between the private and public sectors of the economy would also fade. The ultimate result of the severance of corporate management from ownership would thus be a system of government-guided, if not controlled, managerial bureaucracies that would not be appreciably different from that of European socialism.

The public policy implications of retaining some form of a concept of corporate democracy are immense. Without it, we are left with the vision of the gradual transformation of corporate America into entrenched, self-perpetuating bureaucracies. Some of the economic consequences of ownerless capitalism could be partially remedied by elaborate incentive schemes. Even a number of Communist economies, such as Yugoslavia and Hungary, have tied executive compensation—and tenure—to the meeting of national production goals. Or, there could be instituted some form of a national economic policy, recommended by Robert Reich and others, in which corporations would be assigned priorities and targets. Such measures not only go against the idea of free enterprise, they are unnecessary. A far more feasible solution is to make workable the idea that corporate management, no matter how large or complex its organization, can be fired by owners if it does not perform satisfactorily.

6 / Redressing the Balance

The vital link between ownership and management cannot be restored by attempting to breathe new life into the political metaphor of corporate democracy. In both the Securities and Exchange Act of 1934 and the Williams Act of 1968, Congress tried to impose the language of political democracy on corporate governance, requiring voting procedures, minority rights, and press disclosure.[1] There also have been many insightful proposals made to improve voting procedures.[2] The reason that this approach is doomed to fail is that the electoral model of politics, which depends on political parties, competing candidates, newspaper coverage, and symbolic issues, is not applicable to the governing of corporations. Citizens are an integral part of the political community in which they vote. It is where they typically reside, send their children to school, earn their income, and pay their taxes. If they do not agree with the way it is governed, they cannot easily leave. They therefore have a powerful interest in putting time and resources into the political processes. Shareholders in a corporation, on the other hand, have no such irrevocable connection. They have bought their shares in it as a investment they hope will be profitable. If they do not agree with the way it is being run, they can simply sell their shares, and invest in another corporation. There is not necessarily any economic rationale for them to spend time and money attempting to change corporate government. In practical terms, share holdings in thousands of companies, dispersed among tens of millions of individuals, tend to be too fragmented to organize around any sort of election campaign. Nor can any sort of judicial review produce this sort of democracy in the business world. Perhaps the courts could do more to protect shareholders' rights in circumstances where they are egregiously trampled upon, but the courts lack the business competence or experience to make judgments about the best use of corporate assets. Even if they had the capabilities, such intervention would hardly be consistent with the other objectives of a free economy.

If the political metaphor cannot produce the desired link between owners and managers, then the continued focus on the symbolic sops to democratic traditions, such as "one share, one vote" proxies, only serves to distract public attention from the problem. Shareholders should not be led to believe they have elective power when that is, in reality, a myth. Nor does the judicial metaphor hold any real promise, especially after the race to the bottom, of forcing managers or directors to act as trustees. The only remaining mechanism for making management responsive to owners is the economic sanction: a free and unfettered market in corporate control. Shareholders can realistically discipline management, as Henry G. Manne has rightly argued, if they can threaten to transfer control of their company to other managers. To achieve this end, owners need to have the power, as well as the theoretical right, to sell their control to anyone who can maximize this benefit.

At present, such a free market has been all but stifled by the thicket of corporate defenses devised by corporate law firms. Practices such as paying green mail (or lollipops) to selected shareholders, dispensing manipulative poison pill rights, optioning off the company's assets in crown jewel lockups, arranging for white knights to buy blocks of stock, and stacking the cards against outsiders through supermajorities, staggered boards, and multiple-voting stock have been designed to prevent any real contest for corporate control. Since the Delaware court upheld the poison pill in November 1985, there have been few hostile takeovers; and passed or pending legislation in a dozen states threatens to permanently end this possibility. These state laws further exempt directors from any need to be responsive to shareholder approval and intensify the drift toward ownerless capitalism.

If this trend is to be arrested, and corporate management again made responsible to corporate owners, a free market in corporate control must be reestablished. This would require federal legislation giving shareholders a right they assumed, not without reason, they already had: the right to sell their shares, without uncalled-for management interference, to anyone who offers a satisfactory price. In order to assure that this market is fair and uncoercive, the legislation should stipulate:

1. Any tender offer made by management to any one shareholder would be made to every shareholder on the same terms. This would make any benefit the corporation dispersed indivisible. By doing so, it would

preclude selective green mail and lollipops, as they are prohibited in England and other countries. (In August 1986, the SEC moved in this direction by passing an administrative rule that severely restricted the use of lollipops.)

2. Any tender offer for control would have to be an offer at the same price for all the stock. This would end coercive two-tier tender offers.

3. The board of directors would be obligated to submit all bona fide tender offers for control to the shareholders for a "yes" or "no" vote before it could activate any anti-takeover defenses. Only if a majority of the shareholders approved the anti-takeover defense, which they might if they believed the price was too low, could poison pills and other devices be deployed. This would prevent managements from diluting or reducing corporate assets to preserve control. Since this federal law would supersede state law, managements that took measures to prevent shareholders from exercising their right of control would not be shielded by the business judgment rule from judicial action.

These measures would leave directors, and the management under them, continually vulnerable to competitors bidding for control of their organization. Their tenure would depend, as with employees in any other business, on their performing satisfactorily, which would be measured by, among other things, the price of the stock. This exposure might not make life comfortable for them, or afford them the luxury of running the business as a quasi-public institution, but it would give them a powerful motive to maximize the value of the capital invested in their charge.

Since the market price of shares reflects the expected future, as well as current, return on capital, management would constantly find new ways and technologies to enhance the worth of their shareholders' capital. The resulting free market in corporate control admittedly would increase the risk of dislocations for management, and inspire demands for higher executive compensation (or more golden parachutes), but this would be a small price to pay for restoring the American idea—in substance if not in form—of corporate democracy.

Notes

Chapter 1

1. Edgar v. Mite, 102 Supreme Court 2629 (1982). See also "The Supreme Court, 1981 Term," *Harvard Law Review* 96 (1982):62-71. The SEC came to the same conclusion in "Shark Repellents and Stock Prices: The Effects of Anti-Takeover Amendments Since 1980," Office of the Chief Economist, July 1985, p. 5, note 7.
2. Adolph A. Berle and Gardiner C. Means, *The Modern Corporation and Private Property* (New York: Macmillan Co., 1933).
3. See Edward S. Mason, *The Corporation in Modern Society* (Cambridge, Mass.: Harvard University Press, 1959) for a review of the literature.

Chapter 2

1. Senate Committee on Banking, Housing and Urban Affairs, *Impact of Corporate Takeovers,* Hearings, 99th Cong., 1st sess., June 4, 1985, p. 1111.
2. Ibid., p. 1112.
3. Comments by Ruddick C. Lawrence, vice president, to Board of Governors of the New York Stock Exchange, November 23, 1954, regarding advertising and public relations programs for 1955 (New York Stock Exchange Archives). For a brief history, see Peter Eisenstack, "How the NYSE Went Public" (mimeo), November 1985. Also see, E. H. H. Simons, "Listing Securities on the New York Stock Exchange," *Modern Capitalism and Other Addresses* (New York: NYSE Archives, 1926), pp. 115-16.

48 / WHO OWNS THE CORPORATION?

4. NYSE Archives, advertising file, 1946.
5. Ibid.
6. G. Keith Funston, "America Embraces a People's Capitalism," pamphlet, October 25, 1956.
7. Funston, "New Steps to Strengthen the Rights of Share Owners," NYSE Archives, June 4, 1957.
8. James J. Needham, "Corporate Responsibility Toward the Market System," speech, NYSE Archives, December 7, 1972.
9. Needham, "Who Owns American Business?" NYSE Archives, November 11, 1975.
10. U.S. Senate, *Impact of Corporate Takeovers*, p. 1112.
11. Ibid., p. 1171.
12. Ibid., pp. 1170-71. The same essential argument has been made by John Whitehead, a former director of the NYSE, who noted "the one-share, one-vote principle has long been a cornerstone of this corporate democracy. If it is taken away or watered down, investors will feel that the cards are stacked against them. . . ." See Whitehead, "Don't Bend the Big Board's Rules," *Fortune* (March 18, 1985).
13. First National Bank of Boston v. Bellotti, 435 U.S. 765, 794 (1977).
14. Medical Committee for Human Rights v. SEC, 432 F.2d 659 (1970).

Chapter 3

1. See Appendix A.
2. See Appendix B.
3. Medical Committee For Human Rights v. SEC, op. cit.
4. William L. Cary, "Federalism and Corporate Law: Reflections Upon Delaware," *The Yale Law Review* 83, No. 4 (March 1974):664.
5. Cary, "Federalism and Corporate Law," p. 705.
6. Ibid., p. 663.
7. Lindsey Gruson, "Tiny Delaware's Corporate Clout," *The New York Times,* June 1, 1986, p. F4.
8. Cary, "Federalism and Corporate Law," pp. 690-91.
9. David A. Tanner, "Use of the Business Judgment Rule," *Annual Review of Amerian Law* (1983):51.
10. W. Fletcher, *Cyclopedia of the Law of Private Corporations* (Chicago: Callaghan & Co., 1984), p. 1039.
11. Panter v. Marshall Field & Company, 646 F.2d 271 (7th Cir. 1981).
12. See Unocal v. Mesa, 493 a.2d 946 (Del. 1985); Moran v. Household International, 500 a.2d 1354; Treadway Companies v. Care Corporation, 717 F.2d 757 (2d Cir. 1983); and Panter v. Marshall Field & Company, op. cit.

13. GM Sub. Corp. v. Ligget Group, Inc. (April 25, 1980).
14. Johnson v. Trueblood, 629 F.2nd 287 (3rd Cir. 1980).
15. Panter v. Marshall Field & Company, op. cit.
16. Panter v. Marshall Field & Company, 486 F. Supp. 1168.
17. Panter v. Marshall Field & Company, U.S. Court of Appeals (7th Cir. 1981).
18. Panter v. Marshall Field & Company, 646 F.2d 271 (7th Cir. 1981).
19. Stuart R. Cohn, "Demise of the Director's Duty of Care: Judicial Avoidance of Standards and Sanctions through the Business Judgment Rule," *Texas Law Review* 62, No. 4 (December 1983):591-99.
20. Panter v. Marshall Field & Company, 646 F.2d 271 (7th Cir. 1981), p. 294.
21. Klaus v. Hi-Shear Corporation, 528 F. 2d 225 (1975).
22. Norlin Corp. v. Rooney Pace, Inc., 744 F.2d 255 (2d Cir. 1984).
23. Edward F. Greene and Alan Palmiter, "Business Judgment Rule Tightened For Takeovers," *Legal Times* (January 20, 1986). For the case of Revlon, see MacAndrews & Forbes Holding v. Revlon, Inc., No. 8126 Del. Chan., New Castle County (October 23, 1985). The same limit was applied to a similar takeover device used by the management of SCM. See Hanson Trust PLC v. ML SCM, Nos. 85-7951, 85-7953 (2d Cir. 1986).
24. MacAndrews & Forbes Holdings v. Revlon, Inc., op. cit.
25. Smith v. Van Gorkom, 488 A.2d 858 (Del. 1985).
26. See Bayless Manning, "Reflections and Practical Tips on Life in the Boardroom after Van Gorkom," *Business Law* 47, No. 1 (November 1985):1-6.
27. Daniel R. Fischel, "The Business Judgment Rule and the Trans Union case," *The Business Lawyer* 40, No. 4 (August 1985):1437ff.
28. IRRC Corporate Governance Service, "Limiting Director Liability," July 1986.
29. "Myths and Reality," *Corporate Governance: Past and Future,* ed. Henry G. Manne (New York: K. C. G. Productions, 1982), p. 135.
30. Ibid.
31. Henry G. Manne, "Mergers and the Market for Corporate Control," *Journal of Political Economy* LXIII, No. 2 (April 1965):112.
32. The thesis that the market is inefficient in reflecting the values of corporations has been put forth by Professor Louis Lowenstein. See his testimony in Senate Hearings, *Impact of Corporate Takeovers*, April 3, 1985, p. 112.
33. Ibid. p. 1092.
34. IRRC, *Corporate Governance Bulletin* (March 1985):25.
35. James E. Heard, "Voting By Institutional Investors on Corporate

Governance Issues" (mimeo), September 1984, p. 9.
36. IRRC, *Corporate Governance Bulletin* (December 1985):97.
37. Ibid.
38. IRRC, *Corporate Governance Bulletin* (June 1986):25-27.
39. Interview with Sir James Goldsmith, January 1986.

Chapter 4

1. See Appendix D.
2. See the testimony of Martin Lipton, Senate Hearings, *Impact of Corporate Takeovers*, pp. 8-16.
3. Author's files.
4. Unocal v. Mesa Petroleum, 493 A.2d 946 (Del. 1985).
5. IRRC, *Corporate Governance Bulletin* iii, No. 2 (June 1986):22.
6. Senate Hearings, *Impact of Corporate Takeovers*, p. 1089.
7. "Junk Bonds and Other Corporate Security Swill," *Wall Street Journal*, April 16, 1985.
8. Senate Hearings, *Impact of Corporate Takeovers*, p. 676.
9. Ibid., p. 15.
10. Ibid., p. 1103.
11. Ibid., p. 709.
12. Gregg A. Jarrell and Kenneth Lehn, "Takeover Threats Don't Crimp Long-term Planning," *Wall Street Journal*, March 5, 1985.

Chapter 6

1. Ralph Nader did much the same in his investigation of corporate democracy. See Ralph Nader, Mark Green, and Joel Seligman, *Taming the Giant Corporation* (New York: W. W. Norton, 1976), pp. 33-38.
2. Robert Hessen, *In Defense of the Corporation* (Palo Alto: Hoover Institution Publications, 1979).

Appendix A
Proxy Contests for 1984

In thirteen of the approximately 6,000 corporate elections in 1984, dissident groups satisfied SEC requirements and nominated an alternative slate for the board of directors. Note that in five cases, the contest was for only partial control due to classified boards or the existence of dual classes of stock. Elections actually took place in only eight of the cases, since four contests were terminated by settlements and one by a successful tender offer.

TARGET COMPANY/ (Date of Meeting)	DISSIDENTS	MANAGEMENT/ DISSIDENT HOLDINGS	OUTCOME AND COMMENTS
Alexander & Baldwin (4/20/84)	Harry Weinberg	5.9%/23.4%	Settlement. Contest for full control. Major shareholder Weinberg agreed to end contest in exchange for a seat on the board.
Beverly Hills Savings & Loan (2/24/84)	Paul Amir	12.4%/17.1%	Contest for full control. Dissident would have won contest. He and other shareholders decided to accept tender offer from Triangle Industries before proxies were counted.
Carter Hawley Hale Stores	The Limited (Leslie H. Wexner)	5.0%/2.3%	Management won. Classified board. Contest was for two seats. The contest was a last ditch effort after a failed tender offer which

Appendix A (continued)

TARGET COMPANY/ (Date of Meeting)	DISSIDENTS	MANAGEMENT/ DISSIDENT HOLDINGS	OUTCOME AND COMMENTS
			CHH had thwarted by buying back 50% of its common stock and selling 37% of outstanding voting securities to a white knight, General Cinema Corp.
Electronic Associates (5/9/84)	Howard M. Benedek	N.A./5.2%	Management won.
Enstar (6/21/84)	Roy M. Huffington	3.5%/9.6%	Dissident won. Huffington and three allies accounted for 26.6% of the stock.
Equity Strategies Fund (2/13/84)	M.J. Whitman & Co., et al.	1.0%/37.6%	Dissidents won full control.
Florida Federal Savings & Loan (10/24/84)	Committee to Protect Shareholder Rights	1.5%/3.8%	Settlement. Classified board. Dissidents settled for two seats.
Management Assistance (3/14/84)	Asher B. Edelman, Plaza Securities, Arbitrage Securities	6.0%/7.5%	Dissidents won. Classified board. Won four seats.
Mutual Real Estate Investment Trust (6/29/81)	John V. Winfield	0.6%/6.9%	Dissident won. Classified board. Elected four members of the nine-member board (plus one incumbent supported dissidents). 69% of the shares voted for Winfield's slate were on eight proxy cards. 188 of 3,500 shareholders supported him.
New Jersey Resources (2/2/84)	NUI Corporation	4.2%/4.6%	Management won. Contest was initiated to facilitate tender offer by NUI.

TARGET COMPANY/ (Date of Meeting)	DISSIDENTS	MANAGEMENT/ DISSIDENT HOLDINGS	OUTCOME AND COMMENTS
			During the contest, New Jersey passed a law, lobbied for by NJR, restricting utility company mergers, which seemed to render the contest invalid. NUI lost a suit in district court to test the law's constitutionality, as well as the proxy contest itself, which occurred in a haze of uncertainty.
Norlin (6/21/84)	Rooney, Pace and Piezo Electric Products	14.0%/49.1%	Settlement. Really a disguised tender offer masquerading as a proxy fight. Norlin executives tried to keep control of the company by issuing shares to its ESOP and a subsidiary, diluting the voting power of the dissidents' stock and holding the annual shareholders' meeting in Panama. Norlin management gave in when an appeals court struck down its defensive tactics.
Pantry Pride (12/6/84)	Philip Devon Dwight Devon Howard Gittis Patrick Rooney	0.5%/10.7%	Management won.
Thriftimart (7/19/84)	Hecco Ventures, Pacco Ventures, and Andrew P. Pilara, Jr.	.6% Class A, 80.1 Class B/ 7.9% Class A, 0 Class B	Settlement. Dissidents were bought out for 18% above the market price. May have been case of premeditated green mail. Dual classes of stock ensured that dissidents could win a maximum of four of nine seats on the board.

Source: Ronald E. Schrager, *Corporate Conflicts: Proxy Fights in the 1980s*, Investor Responsibility Research Center, 1986.

Appendix B
Selected Green Mail Payments, 1979-1985

DATE OF AGREEMENT	REPURCHASER/ SELLER	PERCENT OF OUTSTANDING SHARES	VALUE OF TRANSACTION (MILLIONS)	PREMIUM OVER PRICE AT TIME OF AGREEMENT
1/22/79	Zapata Corp./Crane Co.	7.4%	$9.0	13.2%
4/26/79	Chicago Pneumatic Tool/City Investing	8.2	14.0	11.8
7/10/79	Shopwell/ Jacques Amsellam	15.8	1.7	35.9
8/30/79	Milton Roy/ High Voltage Engineering	17.4	5.1	15.9
9/15/79	West Point Pepperell/ Gulf & Western	6.0	12.3	9.7
10/20/79	Sherwin Williams/ Gulf & Western	13.5	21.0	21.7
11/5/79	Host International/ General Host	11.3	12.5	18.5
12/5/79	Buffalo Forge/ H.K. Porter	9.0	4.0	17.6
2/1/80	McNeil Corp./ Walco National	9.4	5.6	28.8
2/4/80	Saxon Industries/ Icahn & Co.	9.9	8.1	27.3
2/11/80	Penn Central Corp./ Reliance Financial	7.9	48.0	6.0
4/11/80	Anthony Industries/ Justrite Mfg.	15.2	5.1	109.9
4/30/80	Reece Corp./ Walco National	9.5	3.7	46.1

Appendix B (continued)

DATE OF AGREEMENT	REPURCHASER/ SELLER	PERCENT OF OUTSTANDING SHARES	VALUE OF TRANSACTION (MILLIONS)	PREMIUM OVER PRICE AT TIME OF AGREEMENT
6/3/80	Ponderosa Systems/ General Host	9.4	7.3	29.1
6/30/80	Standard Coosa Thatcher/ Telvest Inc.	7.5	1.6	3.4
7/31/80	Unitrode Corp./ Dynamics Corp. of America	5.8	21.3	16.8
11/13/80	Robertshaw Controls Co./ Gulf & Western	8.4	9.8	21.5
11/21/80	Oxford Industries/ Gulf & Western	7.4	3.9	21.4
11/28/80	Dynamics Corp. of America/ Southeastern Public Service	11.8	7.3	29.4
12/12/80	Treadway Companies/ Care Corp.	33.0	4.4	38.5
12/12/80	Bliss and Laughlin Industries/ Solar Sportsystems	7.4	9.1	17.2
1/21/81	Pratt & Lambert/ Silbe Enterprises	8.2	2.0	7.4
1/27/81	Kennecott/ Curtiss-Wright	13.5	168.0	42.4
2/2/81	Gateway Industries/ Agency Rent-a-Car	29.3	6.0	6.1
2/13/81	Lane Bryant/ Hatleigh Corp.	19.5	21.0	30.5
2/20/81	Columbia Pictures/ Kirk Kerkorian Tracinda Corp.	24.0	121.9	36.5
3/17/81	Chris-Craft Inc./ Reliance Group	9.6	12.0	8.1
3/19/81	Pat Fashions/ Tweedy Browne Inc.	8.8	11.1	6.3
4/7/81	Bundy Corp./ Southeastern Public Service	5.6	2.8	13.3

APPENDIX B / 57

DATE OF AGREEMENT	REPURCHASER/ SELLER	PERCENT OF OUTSTANDING SHARES	VALUE OF TRANSACTION (MILLIONS)	PREMIUM OVER PRICE AT TIME OF AGREEMENT
4/28/81	Collins & Aikman/ Gulf & Western	10.4	15.0	17.1
5/3/81	Foremost Mckesson/ Sharon Steel	9.3	65.2	7.3
5/20/81	Diamond International/ Simpson Paper Co.	11.0	66.0	21.5
6/4/81	Federal Paper Board/ Reliance Group	25.5	74.2	10.3
7/1/81	Hammermill Paper/ Bayswater Realty Investment Trust	10.6	31.1	13.4
7/10/81	Leggett and Platt/ Empire Inc.	8.0	8.0	32.8
9/22/81	Cities Services/ Nu-West Group	7.2	307.0	40.7
11/16/81	L.E. Myers/ Merrival Ltd.	24.0	9.9	60.7
1/21/82	Greenman Bros./ Initio Inc.	30.0	4.8	42.1
2/22/82	First Union REIT/ Unicorp Financial	28.1	46.0	28.6
4/8/82	Security Capital Corp./ Federated Reinsurance Corp.	14.1	2.4	20.0
4/14/82	Fuqua Industries/ W.J. Kornylak, et al.	8.3	6.0	10.0
4/15/82	Morton-Norwich Products/ Rhone-Poulenc S.A.	20.3	135.0	28.9
6/29/82	Hart, Schaffner & Marx/ American Financial Corp.	8.8	20.5	32.3
7/1/82	Kin Ark Corp./ Hinderliter Energy Equipment Group	3.9	0.6	17.4
8/16/82	Polaroid Corp./ Gulf & Western	5.8	46.9	13.1
8/17/82	Simplicity Pattern Co./ Executive Life Insurance Co.	11.3	14.5	34.5
8/23/82	Anchor Hocking/ Carl Icahn et al.	6.2	11.7	28.2

Appendix B (continued)

DATE OF AGREEMENT	REPURCHASER/ SELLER	PERCENT OF OUTSTANDING SHARES	VALUE OF TRANSACTION (MILLIONS)	PREMIUM OVER PRICE AT TIME OF AGREEMENT
9/10/82	Harsco Corp./ Crane Co.	4.9	17.8	13.8
9/14/82	ACF Industries/ Madison Fund Inc.	14.9	49.0	11.7
11/8/82	Del Laboratories Inc./ G. Lindemann	7.7	1.7	14.4
11/8/82	Ferro Corp./ Crane Co.	22.4	52.5	18.8
11/15/82	Todd Shipyards/ Madison Fund Inc. and Bernard L. Schwartz	13.5	28.2	23.1
11/24/82	Amrep Corp./ Reliance Financial Service	7.9	2.7	8.1
12/9/82	Tosco Corp./ Kenneth Good et al.	12.2	49.5	54.5
3/28/83	Management Assistance/ Continental Telecom	15.4	21.9	7.1
4/25/83	Raymond International Inc./Jacobs Engineering Group	9.9	12.5	19.1
6/29/83	Rexham Corp./ DWG Corp.	5.7	6.9	15.7
7/25/83	Holly Sugar/ Jeffrey M. Picower	9.3	7.4	16.8
7/29/83	Berkey Photo/ Nimslo Corp.	16.0	5.5	6.4
8/19/83	Louisiana Land & Explor./Second Crescent Inv. Co.	17.4	186.1	4.8
9/1/83	Superior Oil/ Mesa Petroleum	3.0	167.2	20.0
11/18/83	Blue Bell/ Bass Brothers Enterprises	14.8	90.1	31.0
11/21/83	Gulf & Western/ American Financial Corp.	9.4	210.1	4.9
3/6/84	Texaco/ Bass Brothers Enterprises	9.9	1,281.8	12.0
3/9/84	Southeast Banking/ Jack Burstein et al.	28.3	147.3	45.8

APPENDIX B / 59

DATE OF AGREEMENT	REPURCHASER/ SELLER	PERCENT OF OUTSTANDING SHARES	VALUE OF TRANSACTION (MILLIONS)	PREMIUM OVER PRICE AT TIME OF AGREEMENT
3/12/84	St. Regis Corp./ Sir James Goldsmith et al.	8.6	159.6	40.5
3/16/84	Warner Communications Inc./News Corp. (Rupert Murdoch)	8.6	181.6	41.9
4/2/84	Blue Bell Inc./ Bass Brothers Enterprises	9.9	54.2	38.0
4/5/84	Castle & Cooke/ Group led by Charles E. Hurwitz	13.1	70.8	22.6
6/12/84	Walt Disney Productions/ Saul Steinberg	11.1	325.3	30.6
7/19/84	Occidental Petroleum Corp./ David Murdock	4.8	194.0	41.9
10/18/84	Louisiana Land & Exploration/ Pioneer Corp.	9.1	96.63	23.35
11/5/84	Goodrich/Carl Icahn et al.	4.9	41.0	25.0[1]
11/25/85	Sonat Inc./ Coastal Corp.	—[2]		

Sources: Kidder, Peabody & Co., *Results of Selected Repurchases of Common Stocks,* July 1985; *The Impact of Greenmail on Stock Prices,* SEC, Office of the Chief Economist, September 1984.
[1]*The New York Times,* January 23, 1986, p. D8.
[2]This an example of hidden green mail, in which the issuer takes on some obligation, other than, or in addition to, the repurchase of its own shares.
 Sonat Inc. bought $111.7 million of Coastal Corp. newly convertible subordinated debentures which converted into Sonat stock owned by Coastal. The debentures pay only 8.5% interest. Coastal could make up to $26.3 million. (*Wall Street Journal,* November 26, 1985, p. 7.)

Appendix C
Selected Golden Parachute Payments, 1981-1985

CORPORATION/TERMS	COMMENTS
1981 Mohasco Corp. $400,000 for four executives.[1]	The parachute was triggered not by a change in control, but by the acquisition of 20% of Mohasco's stock by Gulf & Western.
1982 Burnup & Sims. $4 million for seventeen top executives.[2]	No change in control. Parachute triggered by acquisition of 30% of stock by Victor Posner.
1983 Bendix Corp. Total of $15.7 million. $4 million for CEO William Agee.[3]	Triggered by merger with Allied Corp.
1984 Gulf Resources & Chemical Corp. $8.5 million for ten top executives.[4]	Triggered by takeover of the company by a group of dissident shareholders. Reduced by settlement from $12 million.
1985 Revlon Corp. $35 million ($7 million in stock and stock options) for Chairman Michel C. Bergerac.[5]	Triggered by takeover by Pantry Pride.
Signal Companies. $25 million for top executives.[6]	Takeover by Allied Corp. Payment was originally to be $42 million, but was reduced in a settlement with Allied.

Appendix C (continued)

CORPORATION/TERMS	COMMENTS
City Investing Corp. $30 million for top executives.[7]	Triggered by liquidation of the company. Payment reduced from $40 million in settlement.
1986 Beatrice Corp. Total of $18.5 million. $7 million of that for chairman William W. Granger, Jr.[8]	Takeover by Kohlberg, Kravis, Roberts.
RCA $33 million for sixty executives.[9]	Merger with General Electric.
Swift Independent Corp. $10.5 million for twelve top executives.[10]	Takeover by Edwin L. Cox family.

---

[1] *Fortune*, December 13, 1982, p. 83.
[2] Ibid., p. 85.
[3] *National Law Journal*, November 4, 1985, p. 1; *The New York Times*, January 26, 1986, Sec. III, p. 1.
[4] Ibid.; *The New York Times*, p. 2.
[5] Ibid.
[6] *Fortune*, March 31, 1986, p. 66.
[7] *The New York Times*, December 10, 1985, p. D2.
[8] *Fortune*, March 31, 1986, p. 66.
[9] Ibid.
[10] *Wall Street Journal*, February 10, 1986, p. 8.

Appendix D
Companies Adopting Poison Pills
(Partial List: 8/7/86)

In parenthesis is the approximate date of the pill's adoption and other relevant information.

AMF (Pill declared invalid; company acquired by Minstar)
AMR (2/14/86)
Adams-Russell (6/19/86)
Allegheny International (3/7/86)
Allied-Signal (5/30/86)
Aluminum Co. of America (3/7/86)
Amcore Financial (2/14/86)
American Brands (6/10/86)
American Cyanamid (3/10/86)
American President (3/27/86)
Amfac (7/11/86)
Amsted (5/31/85. Company acquired in management-led leveraged buyout)
Anderson Greenwood (3/17/86)
Anheuser-Busch (12/19/85)
Anthony Industries (3/3/86)
Apache (1/10/86)
Armco (6/27/86)
Armstrong World Industries (3/11/86)
Arvin Industries (5/30/86)
Asarco (Pill declared invalid; company remains independent)
Ashland Oil (5/16/86)
Associated Dry Goods (7/2/86)
Atlantic Richfield (5/28/86)
Avery International (1/30/86)
Baker International (5/28/86)
Bank of New York (12/11/85)

Appendix D (continued)

George Banta (7/31/86)
C. R. Bard (10/10/85)
Barnes Group (7/16/86)
Becton Dickinson (4/11/86)
A. H. Belo (3/10/86)
Baker International (5/28/86)
Black & Decker (4/17/86)
Boise Cascade (1/7/86)
Borden (1/29/86)
Borg-Warner (2/25/86)
Bowater (4/22/86)
Bradley Real Estate Trust (4/11/86)
Brown Group (3/6/86)
Brunswick (3/15/86)
Burlington Northern (7/11/86)
Bundy (1/14/86)
Burroughs (3/10/86)
CBI Industries (3/4/86)
CSX (4/30/86)
CTS (3/25/86. Flip-over pill invalidated by federal court; second pill [back-end plan] enacted after ruling)
Callahan Mining (6/19/86)
Carpenter Technology (6/12/86)
Carson Pirie Scott & Co. (3/31/86)
Champion International (3/19/86)
Citadel Holding (4/15/86)
Cityfed (7/22/85)
J. L. Clark (4/14/86)
Colgate-Palmolive (10/15/84)
ConAgra (7/10/86)
Conna (3/18/86)
Control Data (6/10/86)
Corning Glass Works (7/2/86)
Crane (5/20/86)
Crown Zellerbach (7/20/84. Pill triggered by Sir James Goldsmith, who acquired 50 percent of the company's stock and gained control; now company acquired by James River Corp. and Goldsmith)
Crystal Brands (5/23/86)
Cyprus Minerals (5/12/86)
DSC Communications (5/12/86)
Dana (7/15/86)
Dart & Kraft (9/5/85)
Dayco (5/29/86)
Dennison (4/23/86)
DICOMED (5/15/86)
Donaldson (2/21/86)
Dravo (4/7/86)

APPENDIX D / 65

Dresser Industries (4/18/86)
Dynamics Corp. of America (1/30/86)
Eastern Airlines (2/3/86. Acquisition proposal by Texas Air pending)
Eaton (9/27/85)
Economics Laboratory (2/26/86)
Emery Air Freight (6/12/86)
Emhart (3/3/86)
ENSERCH (4/15/86)
Ex-Cell-o (5/23/86)
FMC (2/24/86)
FPL Group (6/17/86)
Federal-Mogul (7/31/86)
Federated Department Stores (1/23/86)
Ferro (3/24/86)
First Mississippi (5/13/86)
Fleming Cos. (6/24/86)
Flow General (12/6/85)
Foote, Cone & Belding (2/26/86)
Fuller (H.B.) (7/17/86)
GATX (5/16/86)
Gelco (5/7/86)
General Host (2/20/85)
General Mills (2/24/86)
General Signal (3/10/86)
Gerber Products (3/19/86)
Gillette (12/31/85)
Goodyear Tire & Rubber (7/2/86)
Great Northern Nekoosa (3/5/86)
Great Western Financial (6/24/86)
Green Tree Acceptance (10/10/85)
Greyhound (4/2/86)
HBO & Co. (7/14/86)
Halliburton (5/21/86)
Hartmarx (1/16/86)
Hayes-Albion (3/24/86)
Hecla Mining (5/9/86)
Helmerich & Payne (1/13/86)
Home Group (1/30/86)
Honeywell (2/19/86)
Hospital Corp. of America (2/14/86)
Household International (8/14/84)
Hughes Tool (1/22/86)
Insilco (1/20/86)
Instrument Systems (4/2/86)
Interco (9/24/85)
Interlake (6/26/86)
International Minerals & Chemical (3/20/86)

Appendix D (continued)

International Paper (12/20/85)
Invacare (8/6/86)
Ipco (1/30/86)
Jamesway (7/14/86)
Jerrico (10/18/84)
Johnson Controls (11/19/84)
Joy Manufacturing (5/20/86)
Kansas City Southern Industries (5/20/86)
Kellwood (6/11/86)
Kenner Parker Toys (4/22/86)
Kerr-McGee (7/9/86)
Knight-Ridder (6/30/86)
Koppers (2/25/86)
Kroger (3/3/86)
Kysor Industrial (4/29/86)
Laclede Gas (3/31/86)
Lamaur (2/20/86)
Lear Siegler (4/9/86)
Libby-Owens-Ford (4/29/86)
Louisiana Land & Exploration (5/28/86)
M/A-Com (7/30/86)
Mapco (6/12/86)
Mark Controls (5/1/86)
Marsh Supermarkets (7/10/86)
Martin Marietta (7/25/86)
Material Sciences (6/17/86)
May Department Stores (2/21/86)
Mayflower Group (5/23/86)
McDermott (12/18/85)
McDonald's (9/14/85)
McGraw-Hill (1/29/86)
McKesson (5/9/86)
McNeil (6/27/86)
Medtronic (4/23/86)
Meritor Financial (7/17/86)
Michigan National (7/10/85)
Midcon (12/23/85. Acquired by Occidental Petroleum)
Midwest Financial (6/18/86)
Mobil (4/28/86)
Mohasco (2/19/86)
Monsanto (1/24/86)
Moore McCormack Resources (5/13/86)
Morrison Knudsen (6/13/86)
Morton Thiokol Industries (3/28/85)
Mosinee Paper (6/26/86)
NCR (7/17/86)
NL Industries (4/25/86)

Nash-Finch (3/24/86)
National Convenience Stores (6/6/86)
National Distillers & Chemical (2/27/86)
National Intergroup (3/4/86)
Network Systems (7/17/86)
Nicolet Instrument (4/28/86)
Nortek (4/2/86)
Norton (6/30/86)
Olin (2/28/86)
Outboard Marine (6/17/86)
Owens Corning Fiberglas (6/19/86)
Owens-Illinois (9/10/84)
PHH Group (3/18/86)
PPG Industries (12/19/85)
PSA (7/2/86)
Pancho's Mexican Buffet (3/10/86)
Panhandle Eastern (3/24/86)
J. C. Penney (1/28/86)
Phillips Petroleum (2/6/85; new plan adopted 7/11/86)
Phillips-Van Heusen (6/11/86)
Pillsbury (1/10/86)
Pitney Bowes (2/11/86)
Planning Research (4/7/86)
Prime Medical Services (6/10/86)
Production Operators (4/9/86)
Purolator Courier (1/30/86)
Quaker Oats (7/10/86)
Questar (3/17/86)
RCA (9/9/85. Acquired by General Electric)
RTE (6/14/86)
Ralston-Purina (1/17/86)
Raymond Engineering (1/13/86)
Raytheon (6/26/86)
Reliable Life Insurance (6/19/86)
Republic Gypsum (5/7/86)
Research-Cottrell (4/14/86)
Revlon (1985. Acquired by Pantry Pride)
Rexham (3/27/86)
Rexnord (5/2/86)
Rorer Group (2/7/85)
Rospatch (4/29/86)
Rubbermaid (6/24/86)
Ryan Homes (7/2/86)
Ryder System (3/3/86)
Safeway Stores (2/13/86. Pill rescinded 7/28/86)
Santa Fe Southern Pacific (1/29/86)
Schering-Plough (11/11/85)

Appendix D (continued)

Scott Paper (7/15/86)
Sea-Land (12/11/85. Pill rescinded 4/27/86)
Sealed Power (6/25/86)
Sonat (1/23/86)
Southwest Airlines (7/14/86)
Southwest Forest Industries (10/23/84)
Square D (1/8/86)
Staley Continental (4/8/86)
Stanley Works (2/26/86)
J. P. Stevens (7/23/86)
Strawbridge & Clothier (5/19/86)
Sun Electric (3/11/86)
Sundstrand (4/18/86)
Supermarkets General (2/25/86)
Sysco (5/14/86)
TRE (5/23/86)
TRW (12/11/85)
Talley Industries (4/29/86)
Tambrands (12/18/85)
Tandem Computers (5/17/85)
Telecredit (6/26/86)
Tesoro Petroleum (11/29/85)
Texaco (12/10/85)
Texas Eastern (3/3/86)
Texas Industries (7/18/86)
Textron (3/8/86)
Time (4/30/86)
Toro (4/9/86)
Transamerica (7/18/86)
Transco Energy (1/8/86)
Transworld (4/23/86)
Travelers (7/11/86)
Tribune (2/19/86)
Trus Joist (5/9/86)
UGI (4/30/86)
UNC Resources (10/25/85)
U.S. Air Group (1/16/86)
USG (3/20/86)
U.S. Home (6/30/86)
U.S. Life (6/24/86)
U.S. Shoe (3/28/86)
Union Camp (2/26/86)
Union Carbide (12/16/85)
United Technologies (12/12/85)
Upjohn (6/17/86)
Valero Energy (11/18/85)
Viacom International (1/23/86)

Victory Markets (6/5/86)
Wainoco (2/21/85)
Walgreen (7/9/86)
Warnaco (3/24/86)
Westchester Financial Services (12/85. Acquisition by Marine Midland Banks pending)
Williams (1/27/86)
Windemere (6/13/86)
Woodhead Industries (5/20/86)
Zurn Industries (5/19/86)

Source: Investor Responsibility Research Center.